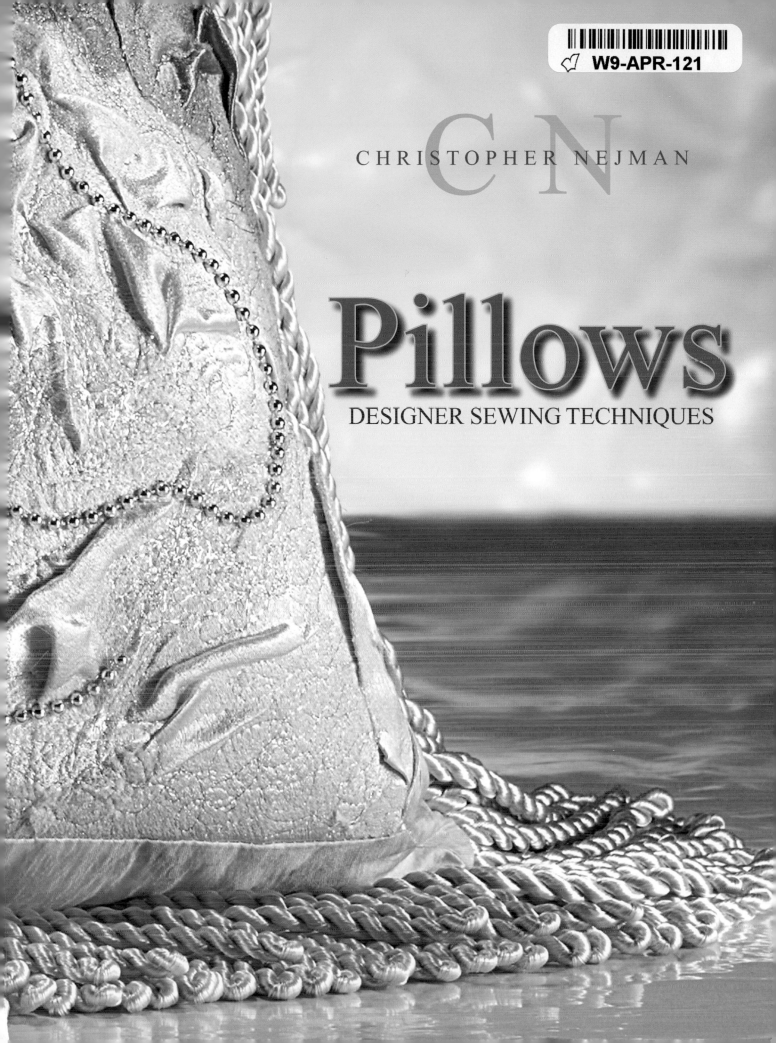

CHRISTOPHER NEJMAN

Pillows

DESIGNER SEWING TECHNIQUES

©2007 Christopher Nejman
Published by

krause publications
An Imprint of F+W Publications

700 East State Street • Iola, WI 54990-0001
715-445-2214 • 888-457-2873
www.krausebooks.com

Our toll-free number to place an order or obtain
a free catalog is (800) 258-0929.

The following registered trademark terms and companies appear in this publication:

A&A Whites, A&E, Airtex, Angelina®, Bernina®, Blue Feather, Brother®, Baby Lock®, Coats, Delta, Dream World, Duncan Enterprise, Expo International, EZ Quilting, EZE-View™, Fairfield Processing, Hobbs, Janome®, JT Trading, June Tailor, Lite Steam-A-Seam®, Mundial Scissors, Nancy's Notions®, Omnigrid®, Olfa®, Pellon®, Poly-Fil, Prym Dritz, Puffy Paint, Robert Kaufman Company, Inc., Sewing With Nancy®, Schmetz Needles, Sulky®, L'orna®, Kandi Corp., Rowenta®, SCS USA, Simplicity, Star Trek™, Teflon™, Tulip, Uniek, The Warm Co., Wrights, YLI

Library of Congress Catalog Number: 2006930837

ISBN-13: 978-0-89689-403-7

Edited by Andy Belmas
Designed by Emily Adler
Photography by Kris Kandler, Mary Collette, and Christopher Nejman

Printed in China

ACKNOWLEDGMENTS

To God, my maker and everything I am and am working to be. He keeps proving to me that when one door closes, he opens a window. As long as he gives me life, I shall keep on creating. Thank you, God, for staying by my side!

To my grandmother, Jadwiga, who gave me free use of her basement to experiment with my hobbies when I was growing up. For all of your love, support, belief and trust in me—and for all the food you cooked to feed all of my friends—I love you, Grandma!

To Sue Ann Taylor, a woman of vision and true professional support, who introduced me to the world on her Internet broadcast: QNN.

To Candy Wiza, my guide at Krause Publications, who supported me and stood by me and listened dearly to my new ideas through this whole book process! You got the true behind-the-scenes look, my friend!

To Andy Belmas, my editor. It's been a pleasure to work with an editor who is kind, patient and able to give clarity to my jumble of words.

To the whole staff and photography team at Krause Publications, who did the beautiful full-page photographs for this book … you rock! To my photo stylist, Mary Collette, your attention to detail is superb!

To Nancy Zieman, who gave thousands of hours and many years of free education on PBS. Without her, I would never have learned to sew!

To Evelyn Byler and Patti Lee at Sulky Threads, who were kind enough to assist me on resolving technical issues with metallic threads.

To Chris Tryon and Steve Jeffery at Baby Lock and Susan Pfaff at Janome, who helped me make this book a successful production. To Shirley Howson and Ron Morella at Brother, who featured my work in their publications, thank you!

To all the companies listed in the resources section of this book. Your assistance and support allowed this book to be produced.

To all the Internet viewers who sent me thousands of emails welcoming my new methods in sewing.

To my immediate family, who helped me through all of life's adventures! I love you Mom, Dad, Cathy and Paul!

To Carolyn, my best friend of over 25 years, I love you! You are always there when I need you! To my nephew, Nicholas, for whom I always try to set a great example. Nicholas, remember to work hard with determination, love and honest morals.

To everyone who believed in me and gave me the chance to explore my creative talents. Your support is priceless!

And to you, the reader. I'm going on vacation now, but I'm looking forward to seeing your pillow when I get back!

Chris Nejman

www.christophernejman.com

INTRODUCTION

Sewing was never something that was in my plans. I had studied to be a fashion photographer and make up artist while earning a graphic arts degree and working a full-time job at a large corporation. I worked from sunup to sundown. Eventually, I opened my very own photography studio; first in my grandmother's basement, then in my own home, and, finally, in an open storefront.

Several years later I took a job transfer and moved to Florida, the Sunshine State. I loved the palm trees, beaches, dolphins and oranges! (Hurricanes never dawned on me at the time!)

After arriving in Florida, I began to miss my creative hobbies. Living in an apartment, I found I didn't have enough space. So I ventured out to buy a home. I visited model homes and really became intrigued with home decorating.

I decided to build my first home, and it was a dream come true! When the home was done, I called upon the local department store to give me an estimate on window treatments. I almost choked on my coffee when the woman told me the price. After she left, I took an immediate trip to the home improvement store, the local department store for a sewing machine and then to the fabric store.

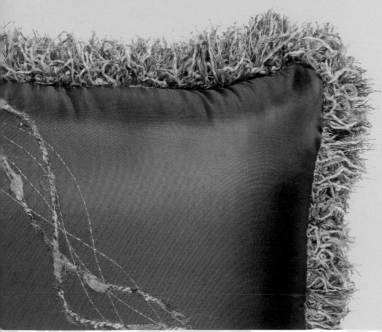

I had tried my hands at sewing years back when velour bathrobes were in fashion. But as soon as I realized how many pieces I had to cut—and when I realized I didn't know how to use my sewing machine—I put the whole bathrobe project into the closet for a future garage sale. I was in too much of a hurry and didn't have the patience to read my manual. I decided sewing was not for me, after all.

Back at my home in Florida, though, I realized home décor was all straight stitching. I knew I could do it!

Soon after, I discovered Nancy Zieman on television showing how to sew. I was hooked!

I was going to a Star Trek convention and needed a costume. It so happened Nancy was teaching how to make a jacket. She was an angel from heaven! A woman I worked with sold me my first serger, and it became the next creative challenge in my life. I made the costume and went back to learning home décor.

After upgrading to a computer sewing machine, I made a basic knife-edge pillow and started to embellish it. With Nancy's help, I learned all about the sewing machine, notions, accessories, presser feet and fabrics … I became addicted!

I tried going to different sewing stores to take classes, but the projects they were teaching were a bit maternal looking. So I turned back to the television and Nancy Zieman became my new best friend!

I like contemporary things, but I respect traditional. We wouldn't have contemporary without traditional. But I needed to have jazzy things, something outside the traditional. So I started to become my own artist and pave my own road. Nancy taught me tools and techniques, and soon I developed my own style!

As you work through the projects in this book, it is my hope you will become your own artist, too. The tools and techniques are all here, but I've left the style largely up to you. This book is designed to help you learn, have fun, take creative chances and develop your own sense of creative freedom. So let's get started!

Table Of Contents

6 Getting Started

7 Sew Like Nobody's Watching

7 The Machine
7 Get to Know Your Machine
8 How Mom Got Her Computer Sewing Machine
8 Mechanical or Computer
9 Tension and Threading
10 Presser Feet
11 Needles
12 Bobbin System
12 Punching and Felting Machines

13 Materials
13 Fabric
14 Thread
16 Trim
16 Yarn
17 Embellishments
17 Closures
18 Interfacing

18 Tools
18 Marking Tools
18 Cutting Tools
19 Adhesives
19 Pins
19 Miscellaneous
20 Pressing Tools

20 Choices

21 Techniques
21 Punching
22 Scribbling
22 Decorative Stitching

23 Projects
24 A Note on the Projects
25 A Harem of Color
36 Beautiful Geisha
42 Eastern Sunset
49 Island of Zumbalame
54 Nefertiti
60 Serengeti Sunrise
68 Whisper of Luxury
72 Sands of Sahara
78 Petals on the Nile
84 Ra
91 Bazaar at Babylon
98 Oasis
104 Romance Over Costa Rica
112 Desert Turquoise
119 Tropical Winds
125 About the Author
126 Resources

GETTING STARTED

Sew Like Nobody's Watching

In this book, you will find new inspiration, educational tips and techniques. If you are new to sewing, you will find it easier than you thought. If you are a long-time sewer, it will re-energize your creative mode!

One of the best things I teach you is to be free with the way you move your fabric. Much like dancing, I teach you to let yourself go and move to the music. Get your hips swaying and your body in tune with the beat! Don't be a stiff dancer. Be one with your machine and forget about the rules. When we begin to experiment and push the boundaries of sewing, we are no longer sewers — we are FCAs: "Fiber Construction Artists!"

In this book, you will find pillows you can make with a basic sewing machine. You will find projects for more advanced computer machines. You will find pillows that can be made with a felting machine or device. And, best of all, you will find projects showing how to create using all kinds of fabulous feet.

The Machine
Get to Know Your Machine

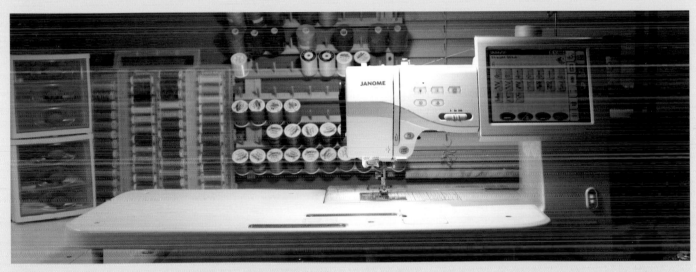

My grandmother was not allowed to date my grandfather because Great Grandmother thought he was of a different nationality. Only after meeting him and spending time with him did Great Grandmother learn he was from the same country as she was. Great Grandmother judged on looks alone, a mistake we should not make with our sewing machine.

That's why I recommend you go on a date with your sewing machine. That's right! Ask your sewing machine to go out with you. Just the two of you. Don't judge on looks alone, take the time to learn.

Getting to know your machine is no different than building a friendship or getting to know the possible love of your life! It takes time to build that relationship. It can be a little easier with your machine, because, unlike people, your machine comes with an instruction manual.

Many new machines come with an instructional CD or DVD. Take the time to watch it. Some people learn visually rather than by written instructions. This is understandable. I myself am a visual learner. I like to watch DVDs to learn.

If you are buying a machine, look for one with a lot of visual education features to help you in your learning process. Try to buy your machine from a dealer who can give you lessons with your purchase.

How Mom Got Her Computer Sewing Machine

One year I went home to visit my mom and dad. I was in my mom's sewing room working with her. I had taken my new computer sewing machine with me for my mom to see. I wanted to buy her one, but she wouldn't allow me to spend the money. So I told her to spend her own money, and she told me my father would not go for it. I asked her why. Dad had just bought a brand new boat for himself! In truth, I think Mom was intimidated by the computer.

So I came up with an idea. We made five pairs of boxer shorts for my dad. My mother could not believe the ease of sewing on my new machine, she was having a ball and got over her fear of the computer!

We presented the boxer shorts to Dad the next day—he asked if they were done on the new computer sewing machine. Of course they were!

After lunch, Dad took us to the local dealer, and he bought my mother her first computer sewing machine!

Mechanical or Computer

Today's computer sewing machines offer you superior creative features over mechanical machines. They provide a wide variety of decorative stitches for hours of embellishments. Because of the increased interest in machine embroidery, more companies are incorporating built-in embroidery hoop attachments for creative, professional-looking embroidery! And the computer's memory can store a variety of decorative stitches.

With a computer machine, there are no more knobs to turn or cams to change—just a simple finger tip on the screen makes your selections. More advanced computer sewing machines have features such as needle up or down, a knee presser-foot lifter, a notification beep to tell you your presser foot is not down when you try to sew (this is great for free-motion embroidery or stippling), a built-in scissors, one-step buttonhole maker and a needle threader.

Even the budget mechanical machines have built-in needle threaders and one-step buttonhole makers. I know from experience that after the age of 40, an automatic needle threader and other helpful functions will make you want to sew more! So choose wisely and select according to your needs. If you are going to spend over $500, your machine better have a needle threader, one-step buttonhole, scissors and a beep to tell you to put your foot down! Not to mention, for the projects in this book, a wide variety of built-in decorative stitches!

A mechanical machine that only does straight stitching can do the best straight stitch over all! Especially if it is a home industrial model, much like some companies are now selling to domestic consumers to use for their quilting.

I use a semi-industrial straight-stitch mechanical machine for all my heavy-duty sewing. This machine has a longer bed extension, so if I wanted to buy a quilting frame, it is the next best thing before investing in a long-arm machine system.

A semi-industrial straight-stitch machine truly has a different feel when it sews. It's fast for power sewers like myself, and there is a real difference in the feeding system. But you still need another machine for all your decorative stitching!

An economy home mechanical machine is a great start for a beginner who wants to learn basic sewing without a lot of bells and whistles.

HINT: For all the projects in this book, I suggest you use an extension table for your sewing and punching machine to support your fabric. If your machine did not come with one, you can order an acrylic extension table from the quilt shops listed in the resources section at the end of the book.

TENSION AND THREADING

Oh, do I remember the day I thought I would make that bathrobe! I had problems feeding the fabric and using the tension system! Today, I realize I was trying to sew too fast.

I got rid of a great mechanical machine because I did not read the instruction manual! What did I do wrong? I kept playing with the tension, and I really did not have to. My thread was not clicked into the take-up lever properly, and my choice of stitch length and foot selection for the thick fabric I was sewing on was wrong.

Tension is really a very simple thing. It allows the bobbin thread and the top thread to balance and make a uniform stitch. When I tried to make my bathrobe, I always got a bunch of thread under my fabric, and I lost my patience. Today, the first thing I teach in a class is to click the top thread into the take-up lever correctly.

The normal tension on a mechanical machine is between four and six. Mine are usually set at four. For heavier fabrics, raise the tension a notch and increase your stitch length. For finer fabrics, decrease the tension a notch and shorten your stitch length. Each project is different. Always experiment before sewing on the actual project.

Most computer machines have an automatic tension system. Follow the threading path guides and you are all set. Some newer, top-of-the-line machines do half the work for you. Run the thread down a simple path and the machine takes it from there. You'll never miss the take-up lever again!

When using metallic threads and invisible threads, you may need to override the tension by threading manually on both mechanical and computer machines.

Take-Up Lever

Presser Feet

Years ago, after I discovered Nancy Zieman on television, I also found Shirley Adams. Shirley was ahead of her time teaching garment construction, embellishments and pattern making. I was intrigued by a foot she was using called a Miraclestitcher made by the Janome sewing machine company. With this foot, you can paint beautiful scenery and add decorative, three-dimensional designs to your projects with yarn.

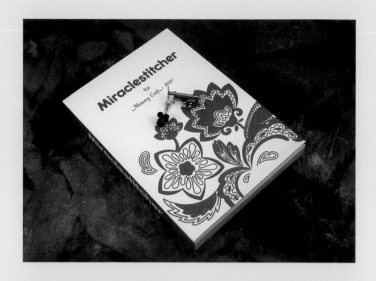

If you're a traditional sewer who only sews a straight stitch and uses only a ¼" foot, your world is about to expand with presser feet! The most important thing to remember about presser feet is that you have choices! Throughout the step-by-step instructions in this book, I will teach you how to use several different presser feet. Each foot will help you perform the different techniques in the book.

HINT: WHEN USING THE STRAIGHT STITCH ON A ZIG-ZAG MACHINE, THE LEFT NEEDLE POSITION BRINGS THE THREAD CLOSER TO THE BOBBIN HOOK SYSTEM FOR A MORE UNIFORM STRAIGHT STITCH.

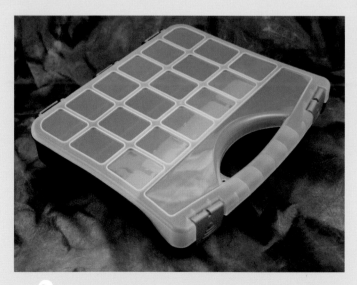

HINT: USE A TACKLE BOX TO ORGANIZE PRESSER FEET.

NEEDLES

Every project begins with the right needle for your thread and fabric. Please, I beg you, before you begin a project in this book, get a new needle. Do not try to sharpen an old needle!

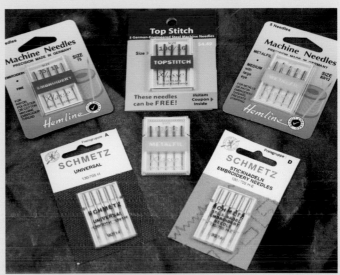

With needles, the higher the number, the thicker the needle. Most needles have two numbers. The first number is the European size; the second number is the American size. Needles are designed to be used with different fabrics and threads. When buying needles, it's a good idea to consult a brand-specific needle chart. Ask at your sewing store and experiment on your own to find the best needles for you and your project.

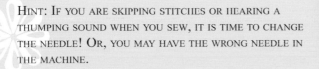 HINT: IF YOU ARE SKIPPING STITCHES OR HEARING A THUMPING SOUND WHEN YOU SEW, IT IS TIME TO CHANGE THE NEEDLE! OR, YOU MAY HAVE THE WRONG NEEDLE IN THE MACHINE.

U.S. Size	Needle Type
9/10	Very fine
11/12	Fine
14	Medium
16	Coarse
8	Very Coarse

Bobbin System

I will spare you the in-depth mechanics and make it simple. There are two types of bobbin systems: horizontal and vertical.

Most of the vertical bobbin systems still use metal bobbins placed in a round metal casing. Some have gone to plastic. The vertical system is under the front of the machine or to the left side.

Horizontal systems use plastic bobbins that are dropped into the throat-plate area. The horizontal bobbin uses a magnetic tension system, so using a metal bobbin will change the way it sews. The only time you will use a metal bobbin in a horizontal system is for bobbinwork, when you can use the weight and the magnetic grip to your advantage.

Each machine company makes a dedicated bobbin just for their machine. Through trial and error, I have found some brand-specific specialty bobbins work for other brands, but the companies do not recommend using them for other machines. If you want to interchange bobbins, do some research and talk to your dealer. An honest, educated dealer will know what machine is made by what manufacturer, and that will help you decide if a brand X bobbin will fit in a brand Y machine.

Punching and Felting Machines

In this book, many of the pillows are made with a technique I call "punching." Punching is basically the same as needle felting, except felting is done with wool while punching is done with all kinds of fabrics. When punching, you are joining a lightweight fabric to a heavier base fabric. In most of the punching projects in this book, the punched, lightweight fabric will cover the entirety of the heavier base fabric. As of this writing, I recommend three sewing machine companies for punching accessories and machines.

Brother makes an attachment for its PQ-1500s straight-stitch machine called the Feltscaper. It consists of a special attachment that fits over your needle bar and a grouping of four barbed needles. The kit also includes a special throat plate and a plastic covering to keep your fingers away from the punching. This attachment also works on the Juki TL98QE and the Baby Lock Quilter's Choice Professional.

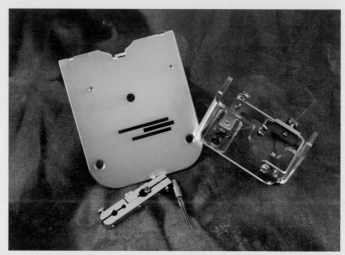

BROTHER FELTSCAPER

HINT: IF YOU DON'T HAVE A MACHINE THAT ACCEPTS A FELTING FOOT, AND YOU DON'T WANT TO BUY A FELTING MACHINE, YOU COULD TRY A HAND-FELTING PRODUCT. I ONLY USE MACHINE FELTERS BECAUSE I FEEL THAT HAND-FELTING IS SLOW AND CUMBERSOME.

The Feltscaper's needles cannot be replaced individually if one should break. You will have to replace the whole four-needle assembly. However, if a needle should break, you can take a pair of wire cutters and cut the broken needle off at the neck of the holding device. You can still punch well with two or three needles.

Baby Lock has a stand-alone punching machine called the Embellisher. It consists of a grouping of seven barbed needles; each needle can be individually replaced if one should break. You can also remove individual needles to accommodate different material widths.

BABY LOCK EMBELLISHER

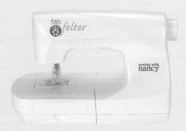

Nancy Zieman has just unveiled her very own felting machine called the Fab Felter. It utilizes five barbed needles that can be changed individually.

HINT: STAY ORGANIZED WHEN YOU SEW. IF YOU HAVE MULTIPLE MACHINES, EACH ONE SHOULD HAVE ITS OWN SET OF FEET, PIN CUSHIONS, BOBBIN-RING HOLDERS, ARM LIGHT AND SEWING AREA. ORGANIZATION LEADS TO EFFICIENCY AND SUCCESS.

EMBELLISHER NEEDLE ASSEMBLY

I recently obtained the new punching machine from Janome called the Xpression. It is a stand-alone machine that features a grouping of five barbed needles and a special plastic guard to protect your fingers. The needles cannot be individually replaced.

I am certain that more punching machines and attachments will become available in the future.

HINT: WHEN PUNCHING, USE A BASE FABRIC LIKE A MEDIUM, BEEFY-WEIGHT, TIGHTLY WOVEN COTTON DUCK CLOTH. THE DECORATIVE TOP FABRICS TO BE PUNCHED ONTO THE BASE FABRIC SHOULD BE LIGHTWEIGHT.

MATERIALS
FABRIC

Quilters, home decorators and garment constructors all have one thing in common: our love of fabric!

For the punching techniques in this book, you will start with a good, beefy-weight cotton base fabric like duck cloth or twill or even cotton canvas.

Punch lightweight fabrics onto the base fabric. Use lightweight fabrics such as silks, suede-back satins, thin satins, lamés, sheers, organzas, silk dupioni, eye-lash fabrics, cotton quilting material, batiks, metallics, lightweight polyester or any other lightweight materials. You can even use old silk scarves.

Oftentimes I'll suggest you buy ⅛ yd. of fabric, which you'll cut into 3" or 4" strips. As an alternative, you can substitute scraps you already have on hand. Here is where you can use all those leftover satins. And if you do go out and buy the fabric, make sure you save your scraps for future projects! Lightweight silks and satins are the best choices for beginners.

When cutting pieces for pillows like A Harem of Color and Beautiful Geisha, don't cut straight squares and lines. Instead, cut the strips into smaller abstract shapes—this will help give your pillow extra pop and visual interest.

Organic fabrics work best for texture, however, polyesters and poly blends give a whole different type of texture. The lighter the weight of fabric you are punching down, the more it will texture! Test and see! Fabric blends play a key roll in creating punching textures.

For the cloth to be punched, do not use heavyweight fabrics such as denim, synthetic suede, tapestry material, upholstery material, heavy brocades, and, by all means, do not attempt to punch leather! Use a medium- to heavy-weight denim or duck as your base.

Remember that these pillows are all about artistic freedom. You are a Fiber Construction Artist — you can look at the fabric I used for each pillow and choose something completely different. I encourage you to substitute and experiment with all kinds of fabrics, colors, sizes and techniques. Experimentation is the best way to develop your own unique style!

THREAD

I use a large variety of decorative threads to embellish my pillows. Rayon thread gives a softer sheen when you do not want a glitzy look to your pillow. Metallic threads are great for glitz. Again, you have plenty of choices, so experiment to your taste.

My computer machines love metallic and invisible threads, but most mechanical machines spit them out. However, one of my mechanical machines does adapt well. Experiment and sew half speed with decorative metallic threads. They are not as strong as construction thread and are meant to be used for decorative stitching. If you are thinking about buying a computer sewing machine, test drive it at your dealer with some metallic thread.

If you use flat metallic threads, use a horizontal adaptor so the thread unwinds from the side, not the top. Think of the way toilet paper unwinds. The flat metallic threads have to stay flat as they feed. On some machines, you will even bypass the first entrance of your thread path with flat metallic thread (see page 15).

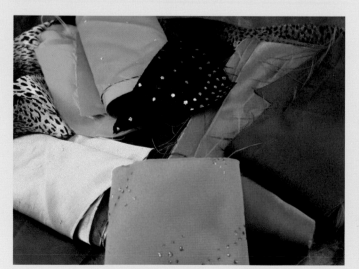

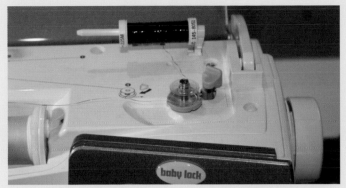

One of my machines has a rear horizontal spool holder. I use an empty bobbin as a guide for the metallic ribbon thread. On this type of machine, bypass the first thread path entrance (the metal hook) as shown.

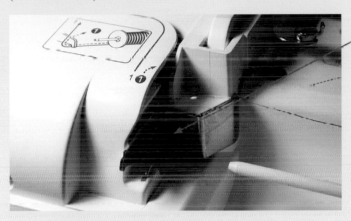

For other machines, I created a device using a plastic-coated wire hanger. If you have a machine that has a similar top (see photo below), you can use a bent coat hanger for your thread. Again, use an empty bobbin as a guide to keep the thread flat. I devised this attachment because most machine companies still do not make a horizontal spool holder for this type of specialty thread. Most machines I own accommodate this homemade device.

WRAP THREAD AROUND EMPTY BOBBIN

Use a 90/14 or 80/12 top-stitch needle when sewing with the flat metallic threads. If your thread runs rough or breaks, you can apply Sewer's Aid Lubricant to the spool of thread. Check with your dealer to be sure this will not cause problems with your machine's tension system. For metallic threads, I usually reduce my tension to about 1.8. Experiment with a test fabric first.

HINT: THE HIGHER NUMBER THE THREAD, THE FINER IT IS. A STANDARD RAYON THREAD IS 40 WEIGHT.

Bypass First Entrance

Use a lightweight bobbin thread when doing decorative stitching. You do not want a heavyweight thread under your fabric, it will cause a traffic jam when doing tight decorative stitching.

You will need a construction thread to finish your projects. If you choose to top stitch your pillow closed, you will want a construction thread that will match the color of your pillow. There are many colors and brands waiting for you at your local sewing supply store!

You'll want invisible thread for select projects in this book to couch yarns, pearls and cording.

TRIM

Trim is the icing on your pillow-project cake! Fabric stores are loaded with these frilly, fuzzy fibers in every shape, color and style. Even retro bead trims bring an elegance to sewing. If you can, select home décor trims. The seam allowance on home décor trim is wider and much easier to use.

I use several different trim sizes and weights on the pillows in this book. The type of trim you use for a pillow plays an important role in deciding on a closure technique. Light, fringy trims work well with a typical invisible zipper closure. Heavy, braided trims, though, require a special zipper treatment, which I will show you later in the book. As with all parts of the pillows, feel free to use different types of trim material. Remember you are the artist, and the choices are yours to make.

YARN

Have you walked through a yarn department at your local fabric or quilting store? My gosh, some of the fancy yarns are works of art on their own!

One day I had my shopping cart loaded with yarns I could not resist. As I was wheeling my cart through the store, a gentleman walked up to me and began a conversation over the yarn in my cart. He told me he started knitting when Rosie Greer, the football player, said it was OK for guys to knit.

He found it kept his hands moving and helped his arthritis. I kindly explained I was not a knitter and told him what I was doing with all the yarn. His wife walked over and she ended up buying some yarn to use in her sewing projects!

I hadn't been paying much attention to prices as I talked and shopped, and when I got to the check out, I was in for a surprise. The average price was eight dollars each. Did I put the yarn back? No! I pulled out my credit card and paid the bill of almost two hundred dollars! But when I got home and added the beautiful yarns to my projects, they looked like a million dollars!

EMBELLISHMENTS

My pillows would not exist without embellishments: pearls by the yard, fancy trims, beads, mirrors, even old jewelry.

Years back, traditional quilters would never couch embellishments onto their quilts. Maybe an appliqué, but that was all. Today, you see tons of embellishments, especially hot-fixed Swarovski crystals. Several companies even make crystals you can iron on with a household iron.

CLOSURES

Invisible zippers are a professional-looking option for closing the bottom side of your pillow. If you take that extra step to put in an invisible zipper, you will not have to wrestle the stuffed pillow under your presser foot. For years, I top stitched my pillows closed. Then I discovered how much more professional it looks to insert a zipper instead.

Sometimes the thickness of the fabric or trim will not allow you to insert an invisible zipper the way it was meant — so you fudge. Heavy, bulky fringes need a zipper sewed on with a narrow straight-stitch foot. For lighter fringes, the zipper can be sewed on with an invisible zipper foot. Or, you can use a hook-and-loop closure method if you are still not comfortable inserting a zipper. Practice does make perfect, so be patient with the new technique.

If you have problems top stitching the pillow under the sewing machine, try using the four-letter-word method: HAND. Yes, you can sew your pillow closed by hand with an upholstery needle.

If you decide to use a pillow form for an everyday pillow, inserting a zipper is essential so you can take the form out to wash your pillow. If you use a fiberfill stuffing like I do — most of my pillows are decorative art pillows, not pillows to lay on — the invisible zipper will give that final, professional finish.

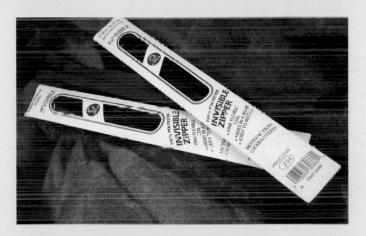

Again, experiment and use your best judgment. No method is ever wrong! When purchasing an invisible zipper, buy one that is three-quarters the width of your pillow. It is important to have this extra room not only for stuffing, but also for turning your pillow right side out.

HINT: TO CARE FOR YOUR PILLOW, VACUUM WEEKLY AND KEEP IT OUT OF DIRECT SUNLIGHT WHEN YOU DISPLAY IT IN YOUR HOME.

Interfacing

Some fabrics require fusible interfacing. I mostly use Pellon 911ff fusible interfacing. However, you should experiment to find the type of interfacing that works best with the fabric you are using.

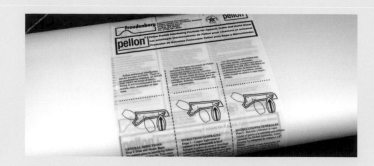

Tools

Marking Tools

Most of my projects do not use a lot of marking tools. However, in some projects I need to draw lines, and a good marking tool is essential!

Marking tools range from chalk and water-soluble pens to pencils and air-soluble pens.

Experiment with the different colors of these tools to find the right one for your type of fabric and project.

Cutting Tools

Sometimes it seems like there are as many cutting tools to choose from as there are fabrics and threads. Start building a collection of scissors, rotary cutters, mats and acrylic rulers so you have the right size and shape in your current and future projects.

ADHESIVES

A good temporary or permanent adhesive is essential to keep fabric, trims and embellishments in place, helping you sew accurate lines for a more enjoyable sewing experience. Test different types of adhesives to discover what is suitable for you!

PINS

Pillow projects require long, sharp pins. I like to use flower-head pins and a professional magnetic pincushion. Be sure to keep the pincushion away from your computer sewing machine screen—it could cause problems with the memory. But don't be afraid. As long as the magnetic pin cushion doesn't kiss your screen, you should be safe!

HINT: AS YOU SEW, BE SURE TO REMOVE EACH PIN BEFORE IT GETS UNDER THE PRESSER FOOT. IF THE NEEDLE SHOULD HIT A PIN AND BREAK, IT COULD CAUSE INJURY TO YOU OR YOUR MACHINE.

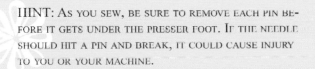

MISCELLANEOUS

For attaching the invisible zipper on pillows with light trim, you will need an invisible-zipper foot. For attaching the invisible zipper on pillows with heavier trim, you will need a narrow straight-stitch foot. If you would like to make your own fringe and trim, you will need a fringe-maker. A circle cutter is helpful for Serengeti Sunrise. And a hot-fix applicator (shown at right) is used to apply embellishments, such as Swarovski crystals.

PRESSING TOOLS

A good steam iron and even a steam press is necessary for a professional finish.

A steam press is ideal to fuse interfacing onto the back of a large pillow base. One hundred pounds of even pressure will guarantee a perfectly fused interfacing!

You can use a standard iron as well, but be sure you have a good powerful burst of steam. Use firm pressure and count to ten when pressing each section, otherwise, your fusible interfacing will not adhere properly. In some cases, you should use a damp pressing cloth.

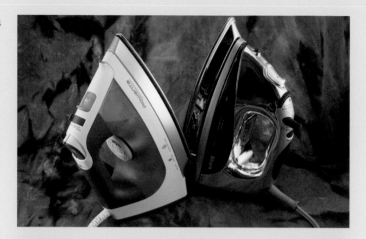

HINT: PRESS YOUR INTERFACING, DON'T IRON. IRONING IS GLIDING THE IRON ACROSS THE SURFACE OF YOUR FABRIC. PRESSING IS LIFTING THE IRON UP AND SETTING IT BACK DOWN ONTO A DIFFERENT SECTION OF YOUR FABRIC, SLIGHTLY OVERLAPPING THE PREVIOUS SECTION WITH A FIRM, EVEN PRESSURE.

CHOICES

Hairstyle and wardrobe choices say a lot about a person. Is this also true of the way we sew? Updating your hair, clothes and even your sewing techniques can be frightening. When we leave our comfort zone, we leave ourselves vulnerable to ridicule or disapproval—but we also open ourselves to personal growth and self-acceptance.

Years ago at a sewing class, one of my students proudly showed her friend her bold new style of sewing. Her friend didn't like it. So my student ripped out all her stitches and started over.

How many of us are trying to please our friends, our guilds, or even our spouses instead of trying to please ourselves? Why is social acceptance more important than our own creative gratification?

People, it's time to create something for you! Have courage and follow your heart!

It is my hope that you will use these projects to sit behind your sewing machine and explore your creativity. I hope you will become free in your heart to be your own person and discover your own artistic talent.

TECHNIQUES

PUNCHING

After sewing for over fifteen years, I discovered something new: punching! Punching is basically the same technique as needle felting. The only difference is felting is done with wool fabric and punching is done on everything from silk to satin to cotton to lamé. This book is the first time punching has been shown as a technique to such a wide audience!

The sewing machine companies have given domestic sewers the ability to felt and punch on a home sewing machine. Using a punching foot has given me far more creativity than I could ever imagine! I can manipulate fabric the way I want without the restriction of sewing and matching seams. Punching is like painting on canvas.

Creating a base fabric by punching fancy, rarely-used fabrics results in a whole new look of crazy piecing. It's so exciting to me, I decided I wanted to share this technique with the whole world!

Not all of the pillows in this book use the punching technique, but if you're looking for a new creative way to sew, I recommend you give it a try!

Felting is not new to the industry. Quilters know about needle-punched batting, but punching is new to the home sewing machine.

A punching foot consists of a grouping of barbed needles that punch fabric down into a base fabric, marrying the fabrics together without thread. After punching the top fabric into the base fabric, if you turn it upside down, it gives a fuzzy felting type texture, hence the term felting.

Punching is like free-motion embroidery or free-motion quilting, but easier. With punching, you can use fine pieces of silk or satin like cotton puffs, cutting or pulling them apart and punching them onto your base fabric. You can also punch yarn to make abstract landscapes, water scenes, sky scenes, dream collages … you can make anything you can imagine. Pillows that use the punching technique are A Harem of Color, Beautiful Geisha, Island of Zumbalame, Whisper of Luxury, Sands of Sahara, Ra, Romance Over Costa Rica, Desert Turquoise and Tropical Winds.

HINT: WHEN PUNCHING, DO NOT LAY THE PUNCHED FABRIC PERFECTLY FLAT. TO ADD TEXTURE, SCRUNCH THE FABRIC A LITTLE; TO ADD A LOT OF FABRIC, SCRUNCH THE FABRIC A LOT AS YOU PUNCH.

SCRIBBLING

In the quilting world, stippling is free-motion stitching without crossing the lines. Meandering is a smaller form of stippling without crossing the lines.

To avoid offending traditional techniques, I will refer to my technique of crossing the lines as "scribbling." In many of my designs, I cross the lines and scribble to cover the pillow top with a lot of metallic thread. This technique looks pretty and helps secure the fabric. The pillows in this book can be stippled or scribbled—I can show you what I did, but the choice is yours.

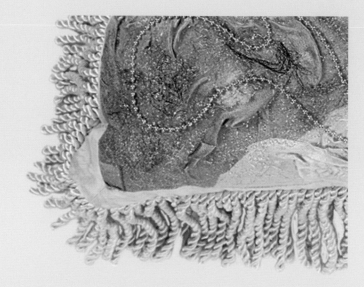

DECORATIVE STITCHING

It is a good idea to test decorative stitches before trying them on your pillow. To test, use a scrap of fabric with a stabilizer on the back and a lightweight, machine-embroidery bobbin thread. Replace your foot with an embroidery or satin-stitch foot. Lower your tension (I lower mine to about 1.8) and test a decorative stitch using one of the colors to be sure the stitch is what you would like. If you don't get the desired results, experiment with tension, feet or materials until the stitches look good.

If you are doing a decorative stitch, and the stitch density is not tight enough, some computer machines will allow you to increase the thread density to give more thread coverage without changing the size of the decorative stitch.

If your machine does not offer this feature, try using a top stitch needle with a bigger eye and threading two spools of 40-weight rayon thread through the one needle. You will get greater coverage of thread without sacrificing the size of the decorative stitch. Again, experiment and test, test, test!

PROJECTS

A NOTE ON THE PROJECTS

You can make your pillows any size you would like. The fabrics you will use to punch onto your base are all up to you as far as color and print and size. You are the artist, you make the choices, I am only here to guide you along the way and make suggestions and show you how I do it. You will develop your own tastes and techniques, and choose your favorite styles and sizes to make.

In the following pages, I give you guidelines to follow. Not rules. Life should not be about rules, but helpful supportive guidelines. Doesn't that take the pressure off and sound more fun and creative?

Substitutions and alternatives are encouraged. If you don't have a Miraclestitcher, use a pearl foot. If you don't have a particular piece of fabric, like a shibori-dyed fabric, feel free to substitute another fabric that looks pretty to you! The list of ways to customize and personalize the projects in this book is endless!

For most pillows, I call for several 3" or 4" strips of fabric. If you are going to buy fabric for one 3" or 4" strip, ask the fabric store to cut a 3" or 4" strip for you. If they won't do that, ⅛ yd. will suffice for one strip. The strips should generally be the length of the fabric (usually 42"-45"), but you probably won't use the entire length. For some pillows, I cut the strips into smaller, abstract shapes — straight squares and rectangles are too boring for me! For other pillows, I begin punching with the entire strip intact and then cut off what I don't need. On some pillows, ¼ yd. of certain fabrics will be needed. Please remember that if you do choose a different size, some of your material yardage will change. For instance, to find the exact yardage of commercial fringe you'll need, measure the circumference of the pillow top fabric and add 2".

A HAREM OF COLOR

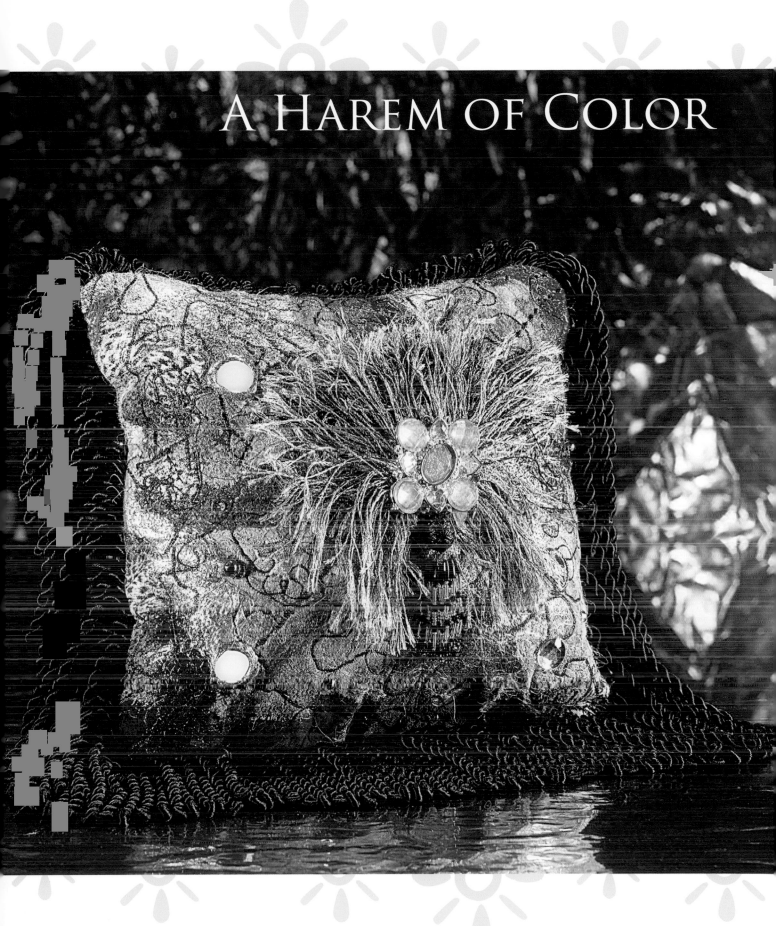

MATERIAL IDEAS

* 12" x 14" piece of duck cloth for base
* 12" x 14" piece of fabric for pillow back
* 3" or 4" strips or scraps of lightweight fabric (10 total) such as:
  * Satin
  * Silk
  * Cotton
  * Eyelash satin
  * Lamé
* Fusible fiber
* Fusible interfacing
* Gold metallic ribbon thread
* Opalescent metallic thread
* Rayon thread
* 4 colors of metallic serger thread for trim
  * Or 1½ yd. commercial braided trim (6" wide)
* Commercial tassel
* Craft glue
* Metallic fabric paint
* Craft mirrors
* Brooch
* Hook-and-loop tape (non-adhesive)
* Painter's masking tape
* Fiberfill

THIS PILLOW WAS ONE OF THE VERY FIRST PUNCHING DESIGNS I CREATED. IT IS A GOOD WAY TO LEARN THE PUNCHING METHOD USING FABRICS INSTEAD OF YARNS. I CREATED THIS NEW METHOD WHEN I BOUGHT A PUNCHING ATTACHMENT FOR MY MACHINE AND ASKED MYSELF WHY I SPENT ALL THAT MONEY ON AN ATTACHMENT THAT JUST PUNCHED YARN. SO I SAT AT MY MACHINE, EXPERIMENTED AND THE REST IS HISTORY!

BASE

1. Start with a 12" x 14" piece of duck cloth as your base fabric, or, since you are the designer, choose another size. The suggested sizes and materials are only guidelines, not rules. (Keep in mind, different size pillows will require different amounts of material.)

2. Next, select nine or 10 lightweight fabrics — I used satin, satin silk, eyelash satin and a lamé. Cut the fabrics into 3" or 4" strips. If you wish, cut the strips into smaller, random shapes before punching.

HINT: IF IT DRAPES SOFTLY IN YOUR HANDS, YOU FOUND THE RIGHT FABRIC.

3. Place your base cloth under the machine. Place a 3" or 4" piece of fabric on the base fabric and begin to punch it down. Begin punching at a slow speed, working your way up to a medium speed. Move in a consistent motion—back and forth, side to side, or in small, circular rotations. Get to know the feel of the punching attachment. Rapid turning, moving too fast and using a too-heavy fabric can cause a needle or several needles to break.

4. When you're done punching the first piece, cut off any excess fabric.

TEXTURE IS MADE AS YOU PUNCH, CHANGING THE LOOK OF THE FABRIC.

5. Keep adding more pieces of fabric around the first piece. Lay out the fabric strips the way you want, or use the photo at the beginning of the project as a guide. You are the artist, you design it the way you want to!

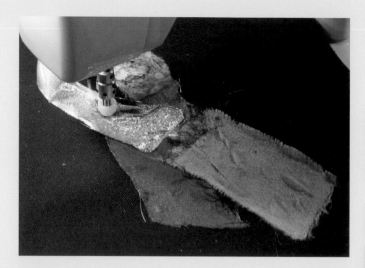

7. Next, pull out some thin strands of a fusible fiber (I recommend Angelina). Place the fibers on top of the punched material, and punch them into the fabric.

6. Keep adding pieces of fabric, cutting off the excess as you go, until you have covered your whole base fabric. Remember, punch at a consistent, medium speed and do not turn fast! If you use lamé fabric, do not punch over it too much for this will cause it to fray. In some cases we want fraying, but not on this beginner technique. For more texture, scrunch the fabric as you punch.

HINT: PUNCH THE EDGES WELL TO FEATHER ONTO THE NEXT PIECE OF FABRIC.

8. Turn the fabric over on your cutting mat, and cut off the excess fabric around your base using an acrylic ruler and rotary cutter.

10. Turn everything upside down and place on the bed of your steam press. You can also use an iron if you do not have a steam press.

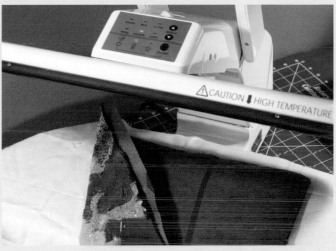

9. Turn your base right side up. Place it on top of fusible interfacing with the dotted-glue side up. Cut the interfacing around the pillow to size. I am using Pellon's 911ff non-woven fusible interfacing. This is a great interfacing for my pillows, especially because we will be doing a lot of decorative stitching. You can choose to use two layers if you wish for firmer support. I find one layer sufficient since there is already so much punched fabric providing support.

11. Cover with a press cloth and fuse.

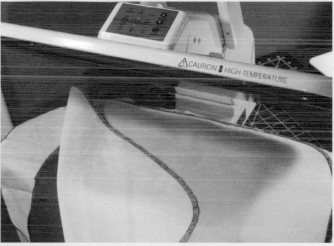

DECORATIVE STITCHING

1. Attach an embroidery or satin stitch foot to your machine, and thread it with a metallic ribbon thread. Engage your feed dogs. Turn your tension down to about 1.6. Remember to test your stitch on a piece of stabilized scrap fabric before stitching on your pillow.

2. Begin stitching medium-wide satin stitches, turning the fabric as you sew for a curly look.

3. Switch to a decorative stitch. When I sew decorative stitches, I like to switch between metallics and rayons. Sew as many decorative stitches as you wish with many different colors and types of shiny threads. I recommend trying many different built-in decorative stitches on a sample pillow top before choosing the ones you want to use on your pillow. Play with the hundreds of stitches built into your machine— this is your chance to use them. After all, you paid for them!

ATTACHING THE TASSEL

1. Take the foot off your machine and drop your feed dogs. Place the tassel near the center of the pillow, making sure it will not hang below the bottom of the pillow. To tack the tassel loop onto the pillow, use a wide zig-zag stitch that passes over the width of the loop.

ATTACHING CRAFT MIRRORS

1. Apply glue in various areas of the pillow to glue down craft mirrors.

2. Apply the mirrors, and then apply metallic fabric paint around the mirrors. At first the fabric paint may look messy, but it shrinks as it dries for a nice decorative look. You may also skip the glue and just use the paint as glue. The choice is yours.

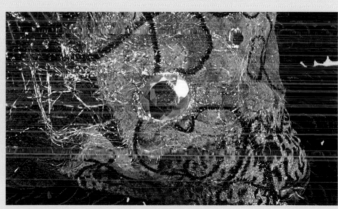

MAKING AND ATTACHING THE FRINGE

1. For the fringe, select four different colors of metallic serger thread (I used Candle Light by YLI). Following the instructions on your fringe maker, wrap the threads onto the machine.

2. Remove the metal wires from the fringe maker with the fringe still attached, and place under your sewing machine. Using a narrow straight-stitch foot, open-toe foot or standard foot butted against the edge of one side, sew straight rows several times to secure the fringe.

3. Remove the fringe from the machine, and cut the loops on the long side of the fringe.

4. Place the fringe above the tassel, and tack it down with your sewing machine. To keep the fringe laying flat when the pillow stands up, lightly glue the back of the fringe to the base of the pillow. Finish by gluing down a jewel or brooch.

ATTACHING THE TRIM

1. Determine which side of your pillow is going to be the bottom by deciding which way you want the tassel to hang. When you apply your trim, it is best to start on the left side of the pillow. In the accompanying photo, the left side is on the bottom. Pin the trim around the pillow, overlapping by one inch. It is important to overlap because the bottom of the pillow will have your opening, and overlapping will prevent a gap in the trim.

HINT: MEASURE YOUR PILLOW TOP ALL THE WAY AROUND AND ADD 2" WHEN YOU GO TO PURCHASE YOUR TRIM.

2. Lay the pillow right side up under your sewing machine, and stitch around the trim on the very left edge making sure all the trim is laying on top and pointed to the middle of the pillow top. Most trims are on the bias, so it is easy to mold the trim around the pillow in the corners as shown in the photo.

THE PILLOW BACK

1. The back of the pillow should complement the front. I like to add a design to the back. We are going to keep it simple for our first pillow. In the rest of the book I will show you photos of the pillow backs to give you ideas on how to design yours. For this pillow, I just crossed an intersection with a simple, decorative wave stitch using the satin-stitch foot.

2. If you want to sign your name on the back of the pillow, sign your name on a piece of paper, scan it, digitize it and load it into your embroidery machine.

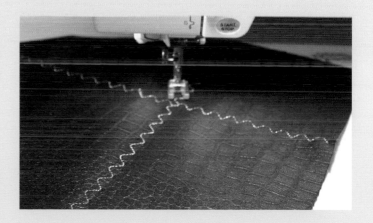

3. Hoop a tear-away stabilizer, and apply a spray adhesive.

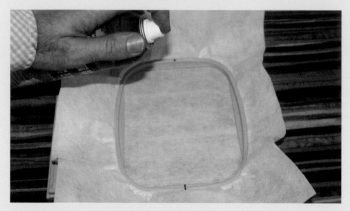

4. Place your back fabric onto the sticky, hooped stabilizer, and embroider your signature. This technique will hold the fabric in place and prevent hoop marks.

HINT: IF YOU SELECT A LIGHTWEIGHT FABRIC FOR THE BACK, IT IS A GOOD IDEA TO FUSE INTERFACING TO IT. A STIFF UPHOLSTERY FABRIC IS USUALLY BEEFY ENOUGH TO SUPPORT THE PILLOW WITHOUT INTERFACING, BUT IF YOU CHOOSE TO DO EMBROIDERY ON THE BACK, YOU SHOULD USE INTERFACING. FOR LIGHT FABRIC, USE LIGHT INTERFACING. FOR HEAVY FABRIC, USE HEAVY INTERFACING.

MAKING THE CLOSURE

1. Lay the front and the back of the pillow facing each other at the bottoms. Cut a piece of hook-and-loop tape, leaving a space for your hand plus 2". Pin the hook tape on one side and the loop tape onto the other side of the pillow as shown.

HINT: USE NON-ADHESIVE HOOK-AND-LOOP TAPE. STICKY-BACK HOOK-AND-LOOP TAPE CAN GUM UP THE NEEDLE AND CAUSE SKIPPED STITCHES.

2. Sew the hook tape to one side of the pillow and the loop tape to the other side of the pillow.

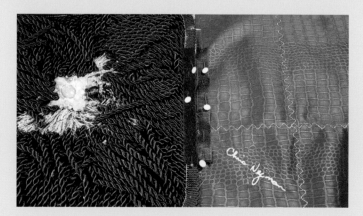

FINISHING

1. Sandwich the pillow right sides together and pin. Leave the hook-and-loop opening unpinned; you will not stitch this part together.

2. Since the trim was sewn onto the top of the pillow, you will now sew with the top side on top. Follow the original thread line from when you sewed on the trim, but move the needle position to the left one thread width, if your machine allows it. Because the top fabric was already slightly eased when you sewed on the trim, you want the bottom fabric to ease as well. I like to use a generous $1/2$" to 1" seam allowance when stitching around the pillow. Most upholstery trim has a 1" band.

3. Now, press open your seams, trim the corners so they are round, and turn your pillow inside out.

4. Stuff the pillow with fiberfill. Pull apart small pieces, like pulling apart cotton candy, so you will have movement and fullness to your pillow. If you are using the hook-and-loop closure, be sure to use painter's masking tape to cover the hook and loop so the stuffing won't stick. After stuffing, remove the tape, and seal the pillow closed!

PILLOW BACK

BEAUTIFUL
GEISHA

MATERIAL IDEAS

- ❋ 11" x 12" piece of duck cloth for base
- ❋ 11" x 12" piece of doe-skin or cotton velveteen for pillow back
- ❋ 4" strips or scraps of lightweight fabric for punching (5-8 strips total)
- ❋ Fusible interfacing
- ❋ Metallic ribbon thread
- ❋ Black embroidery thread
- ❋ Invisible thread
- ❋ Lightweight bobbin thread

- ❋ 3 colors of metallic serger thread
- ❋ 1⅓ yd. commercial braided trim (6" wide)
- ❋ 1-2 yd. pearl strand
- ❋ Craft mirrors
- ❋ Crystals
- ❋ Glue
- ❋ Hook-and-loop tape (non-adhesive)
- ❋ Painter's masking tape
- ❋ Fiberfill
- ❋ Metallic fabric paint

I WANTED THIS PILLOW TO HAVE AN ASIAN FLAIR TO IT, SO I PUNCHED ON 3" AND 4" PIECES OF ASIAN-PRINT SILKS AND POLY SILKS. FEEL FREE TO USE A DIFFERENT SIZE FOR THE BASE CLOTH, AND FEEL FREE TO SUBSTITUTE COLORED FABRICS. YOU MAY FOLLOW THE FABRIC DESIGN AS SEEN IN THE PICTURES, OR CREATE YOUR OWN DESIGN.

1. Cut an 11" x 12" piece of duck cloth for the base, and place it under your sewing machine. Build your design as shown in the first pillow project, punching 3" or 4" pieces of fabric to completely cover the base cloth. Again, you may follow the design as shown in the photo, or create your own design.

2. Turn the base cloth upside down, and cut off excess fabric. Fuse interfacing onto the back just like we did in the first pillow project. You may choose to fuse two layers for added support and a more detailed quilted look.

3. Put on a free-motion embroidery foot, and lower your feed dogs. If your machine does not beep at you when you forget to put the foot down before sewing, always try to remind yourself to do so. Lowering your foot before you free-motion stitch will engage the tension and prevent a wad of thread from forming under your pillow top.

4. Thread your machine with metallic ribbon thread, and set your tension to 1.8. Remember to set your spool of thread in a horizontal position as shown on page 15. Remember to test first and make adjustments accordingly.

5. Coat your whole pillow top with free-motion stippling or scribbling. This will also help reinforce the punched fabric.

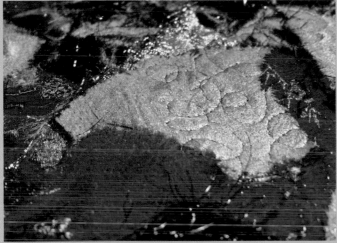

FREE-MOTION SCRIBBLING ON THE PILLOW TOP.

FREE-MOTION SCRIBBLING ON THE BACK OF THE PILLOW TOP.

6. Now thread a black embroidery thread onto your machine. Select one or many different decorative stitches and test the stitches on a test scrap with stabilizer to make sure you get the desired results. I used a leaf stitch.

7. Start sewing on your pillow. You can follow seam lines if you wish, or just sew randomly with different stitches across the whole pillow.

8. Attach a pearl foot to your machine and thread it with invisible thread. We are going to use a zig-zag stitch. Test by hand the width of the zig-zag stitch to be sure it clears the width of the pearls.

9. Randomly sew your pearls on in any direction you wish.

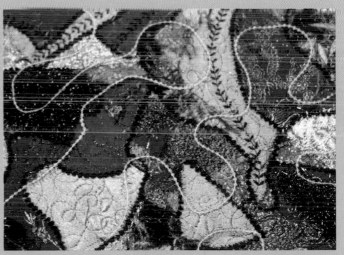

10. Apply crystals to your pillow with a hot-fix applicator following the manufacturer's instructions.

11. Review the instructions for making and attaching fringe as shown in the first pillow project on page 32. Or purchase a pre-made commercial trim.

12. Wrap the metallic serger thread around the fringe maker. This time, sew up and down the middle of the fringe several times.

13. Take the fringe out from under your sewing machine, and cut the loops at both ends.

14. Remove the fringe from the metal rods. Cut the fringe into 3" sections.

15. Form the fringe into a circle on your pillow and tack down.

16. Glue a jewel and attach a crystal to the top of the jewel with a hot-fix applicator.

17. Apply a heavy-corded trim as shown in the first pillow project.

18. Add a hook-and-loop closure and finish the pillow as shown in the first pillow project.

PILLOW BACK

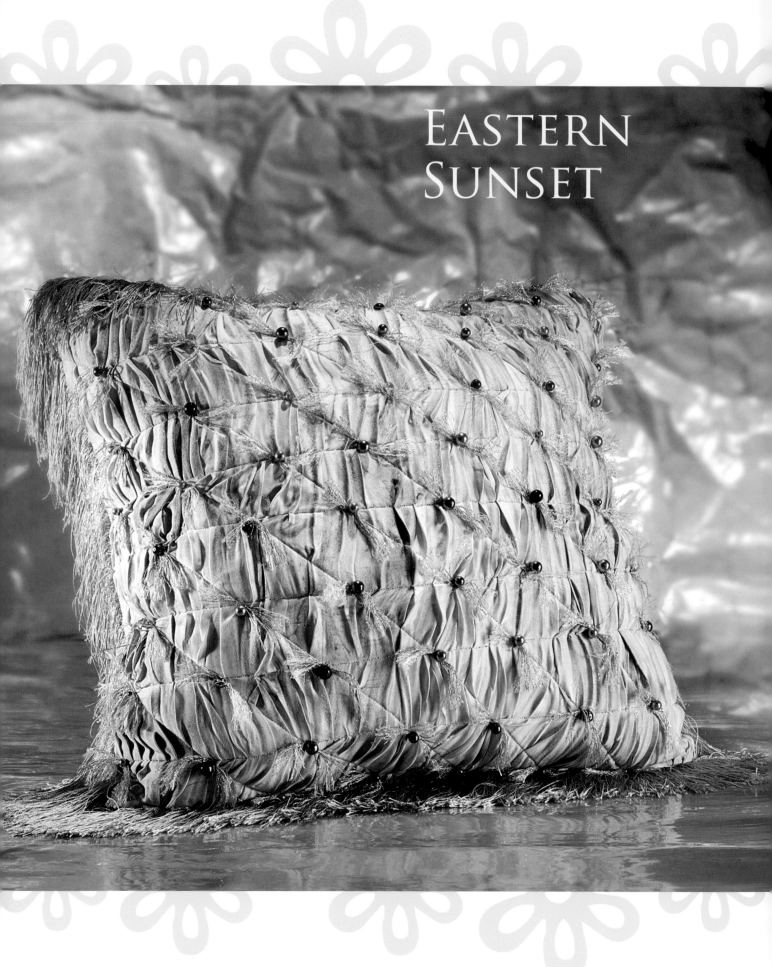

EASTERN
SUNSET

MATERIAL IDEAS

* 22" square Shibori- or hand-dyed fabric
* 22" square fleece
* 22" square fabric for pillow back
* Metallic threads
* Variegated quilting thread
* Metallic serger thread
* Invisible thread
* Pastel beads
* Fusible interfacing
* 2½ yd. lightweight trim (4½" wide)
* Invisible-zipper and invisible-zipper foot
* Glue stick
* Fiberfill

SHIBORI-DYED FABRIC BY LADY DYE

SHIBORI IS A SILK FABRIC PAINTING TECHNIQUE DEVELOPED BY THE JAPANESE. IT IS A METHOD OF MANIPULATING FABRIC BEFORE IT IS PAINTED. AFTER THE PROCESS IS DONE, ONE MUST SEW TO HOLD THE TEXTURE TOGETHER. NOTICE THE PLEATED WRINKLES IN THE PHOTOGRAPH—THE WRINKLES ARE AN IMPORTANT PART OF THE SHIBORI TECHNIQUE.

FOR THIS PILLOW, I CHOSE TO USE AN INVISIBLE-ZIPPER CLOSURE FOR A MORE PROFESSIONAL FINISH.

1. Cut a 20" square of the Shibori fabric and a 20" square of fleece.

2. Pin the fleece to the back of the fabric, or use a temporary spray adhesive.

3. Use metallic threads to sew vertical and diagonal rows of straight stitching onto the pillow top, leaving 2" between rows.

4. Thread a variegated quilting thread onto your machine, and select approximately five strands of metallic serger thread. Cut them to cover the diagonal length of the pillow. Lay the five threads down as one. Use a decorative single stitch to tack the metallic thread down on the diagonal intersections. As an alternative, you can drop your feed dogs and do zig-zag stitches at every intersection.

5. Cut a back fabric the same size as the pillow front. Fuse interfacing to the back and use metallic thread to create rows of decorative stitches.

6. Cut several strands of metallic serger thread. Couch them in place at the decorative stitch-pattern intersections much like Step 4, only this time you're on the pillow back.

7. Attach a light, commercial-made fringe trim as shown in the first two pillow projects. For this pillow, I chose a beautiful lilac-colored fringe.

APPLYING AN INVISIBLE-ZIPPER

8. Take a zipper out of its package. Unzip it and lay it right side down. Use a steam iron to iron the coils open flat.

HINT: WHEN PURCHASING A ZIPPER FOR ANY PILLOW, BE SURE IT IS ABOUT THREE QUARTERS OF THE PILLOW'S WIDTH. A WIDE ZIPPER IS SAFER BECAUSE YOU WILL BE ABLE TO FIT YOUR HAND THROUGH TO STUFF IT, AND IF THE PILLOW IS BULKY, THE OPENING IS LARGE ENOUGH TO PULL THE PILLOW RIGHT SIDE OUT.

9. Butt the bottoms of the front and back of the pillow together and even them out. Mark with a marker or a pin where the zipper will begin on each side. This step is very important. I used a black marker for demonstration. I would normally use pins.

10. Use a glue stick to glue the right side of the zipper tape to help hold it down.

11. Place the zipper right side down on the right side of the pillow back. Be sure the zipper teeth are facing the pillow as shown in the photo below. If you need further help, read the instructions that came with the zipper.

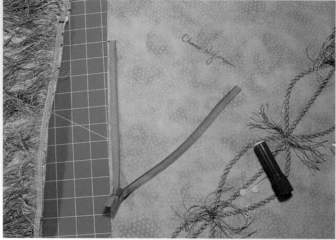

12. Put an invisible-zipper foot on your machine. Mark on your zipper where the teeth at the top of the zipper actually begin. This is where you will start sewing.

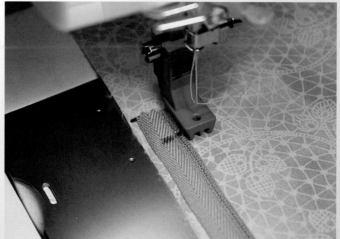

HINT: When attaching an invisible-zipper, the zipper teeth should face the inside of the pillow.

13. Place the zipper teeth under the right groove of the invisible-zipper foot. Sew a couple stitches and then sew back a couple stitches to lock the stitch. Continue to sew all the way down until you hit the zipper slider. Back stitch and remove from under the sewing machine.

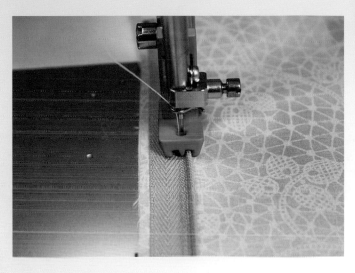

14. Place the pillow back on top of the pillow top, right sides together as shown in the photo below. Place the un-sewn section of the zipper onto the pillow front right sides together.

15. Line up the un-sewn zipper to the pillow front at the mark that was previously made with a black marker.

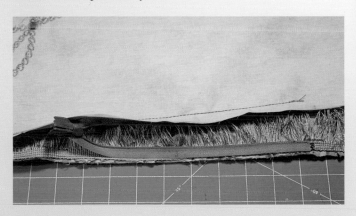

16. Now place the zipper teeth into the left groove of the invisible-zipper foot and back stitch; sew all the way down as you did the first time.

17. Test the zipper to be sure it closes properly. Then close the zipper a quarter of the way. Sandwich your two layers together and pin. At the top of the zipper, pull both end tabs outside the pillow; use a pin to keep them there as shown below. Do the same to the bottom. You will sew these this way.

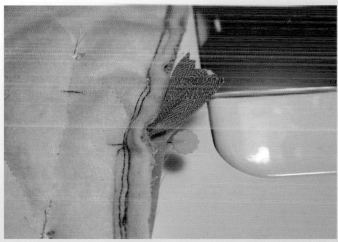

18. Pin and sew around your pillow. Do not sew where the zipper teeth are, but rather start and stop on the tabs. Use the lines of the zipper stitch as your seam allowance around the whole pillow.

19. Turn the pillow right side out. Congratulations on a beautiful invisible closure! In some cases, the trim will be too bulky for this method, but I will show you later how to use a zipper with bulky trim.

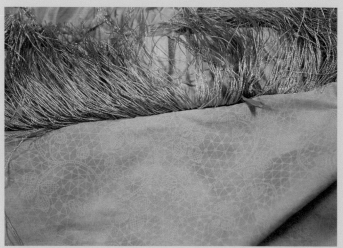

ZIPPER CLOSED

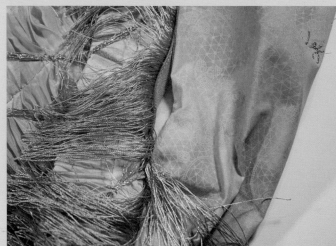

ZIPPER OPENED

20. You can choose to leave the pillow as is, or glue beads at every intersection as I have done. Cut the metallic cords in the centers, and hit them with a little steam from the iron.

PILLOW BACK

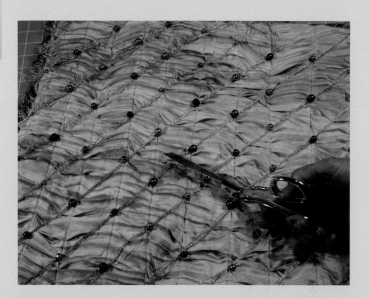

21. Stuff the pillow, zip shut and you have a decorative Shibori pillow!

ISLAND OF
ZUMBALAME

MATERIAL IDEAS

❄ 16" square duck cloth for base

❄ 16" square fabric for pillow back

❄ $1/4$ yd. black suede-back satin

❄ $1/4$ yd. tan suede-back satin

❄ $1/4$ yd. red suede-back satin

❄ Red and black metallic ribbon thread

❄ Black acrylic worsted-weight yarn

❄ 20 wood beads

❄ 2 large wood beads

❄ 2 yd. heavy trim ($2^1/2$" wide)

❄ Invisible-zipper and narrow straight-stitch foot

❄ Glue stick

❄ Fiberfill

❄ Tassel

I GOT THE IDEA FOR THIS PILLOW FROM A BEAUTIFUL NECKLACE ONE OF MY FRIENDS WEARS. IT REMINDS ME OF A DESIGN YOU WOULD FIND ON A TROPICAL ISLAND MADE AND DE-SIGNED BY THE NATIVE PEOPLE. I CHOSE TO USE SUEDE-BACK SATIN MATERIALS IN BLACK, TAN AND RED FOR AN EARTHY LOOK.

1. Cut a 16" x 16" piece of duck cloth for the base fabric.

2. Cut an uneven, 4" x 4" square of the black suede-back satin. Place it in the center of the base fabric, and punch it down.

3. Place a smaller square of the tan fabric in the center of the black. Punch it down.

4. Cut 3" strips of the red fabric. Punch pieces of the strips around the black fabric.

5. Cut the tan fabric into 3" strips, punch pieces of the strips around the design.

6. Cut the black fabric into 3" strips, punch pieces of the strips around the design.

7. Continue building your base as shown.

8. Channel stitch rows of straight stitching in each panel using matching metallic ribbon thread. (I used Sulky's sliver threads.)

9. Next, using a pearl foot and black metallic thread, couch down yarn with a narrow satin stitch along the panels on each side of the outermost black strips. Do not sew all the way to the end of the pillow. Stop stitching approximately ⅜" from the corners, leaving long tails of yarn.

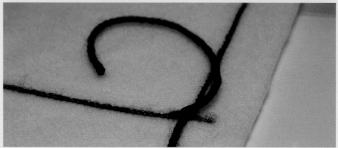

10. At each corner, thread one tail through a wooden bead, and bring the other tail around the outside of the bead. Using both tails, tie a knot to keep the bead in place. I repeated this process four times at each corner.

SHOWN ON PLAIN FABRIC
FOR IMPROVED VISIBILITY.

11. Scribble fabric paint on to the tan fabric. (I use Puffy Paint, a product that is steamed when dry for a puffy effect.)

12. Design the back of your pillow. I applied decorative stitches, tacked down strands of yarn and tied on beads.

13. Apply a heavy, coordinating trim as shown in the first pillow project on page 33.

14. Because the trim was so thick, I could not use an invisible-zipper foot to sew in the invisible-zipper. Instead, I used a narrow straight-stitch foot. The invisible insertion method had the zipper coils too close to the heavy trim I used and would not close (see page 71). This method of closure is perfectly acceptable. The closure is on the bottom and no top-stitching lines show!

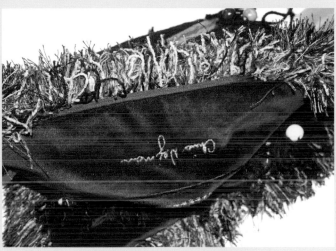

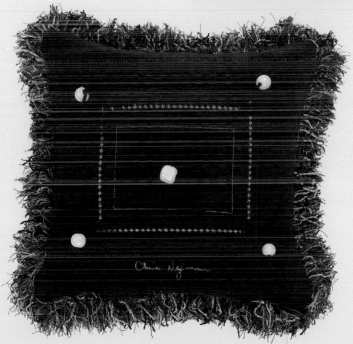

PILLOW BACK

MATERIAL IDEAS

* 18" square black doeskin or cotton velveteen fabric
* $2/3$ yd. black doeskin or velveteen for backing, tubes and side borders
* Gold cording
* Decorative bracelet
* Beaded necklace with pendant
* Invisible thread
* Jewel glue
* Gold metallic fabric paint
* $2^1/4$ yd. lightweight commercial trim ($4^1/2$" wide)
* Decorative yarns
* Decorative metallic serger thread
* Tassel
* Invisible-zipper and invisible-zipper foot
* Glue stick
* Fiberfill

ANCIENT MYTHOLOGY WAS THE INSPIRATION FOR THIS NEXT PILLOW. I HAD AN IDEA OF LAYING DOWN LINES THAT LOOKED LIKE POURED GOLD, BUT I DID NOT WANT TO DO IT WITH SATIN STITCHING. THE STIPPLED LINES OF GOLD WOULD BE LIKE A SNAKE IN THE DESERT OF EGYPT. THE JEWELS WOULD BE LIKE THOSE WORN BY THE MOST BEAUTIFUL WOMEN IN THE LAND. MY MIRACLESTITCHER WAS DESIGNED TO COUCH DOWN YARN, BUT WHAT IF I TOOK CRAFTER'S CORDING AND PUT IT IN THE EYE OF THE FOOT ATTACHMENT? TRY IT AND FIND OUT!

1. Start with an 18" square of fabric that looks like velour but is actually a doe-skin finish. Fuse interfacing onto the back for support. Cut an 18" square of fleece to use as the backing, and spray baste it to the back of the pillow top.

2. Using a Miraclestitcher or a pearl foot, couch down the cording in an "S" pattern across the whole top fabric. Leave a 1" space around the edge of the fabric for a seam allowance.

HINT: IF YOU DO NOT HAVE A MACHINE THAT ACCEPTS THE MIRACLESTITCHER, YOU CAN USE A PEARL FOOT OR A BRAIDING FOOT. SEW LONG, SLOW "S" CURVES UP AND DOWN EACH ROW UNTIL THE SURFACE OF THE PILLOW IS COVERED.

3. Cut four strips of the doe-skin fabric, each approximately 2" wide.

FABRIC STRIPS PICTURED WITH TUBE TURNER.

4. Using a tube-turner foot attachment, sew each strip of fabric right sides together with a ¼" seam allowance.

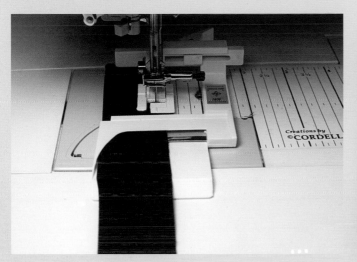

5. Turn the tubes right side out using the tube turner. Select a decorative bracelet. Locate the center of the pillow, and pin four of the tubes equal distance from each corner to and around the bracelet.

6. Sew the tubes flat across and next to the bracelet. Make sure you tack stitch the beginning and end of the stitch.

7. Sew a straight-stitch down the center of the tubes to each corner of the pillow.

8. Go back to your stash of jewels and find a necklace with a pendant or button. Cut the pendant off and glue it to the center of the bracelet. Take the necklace apart, and evenly distribute the beads down each of the tubes with jewel glue. Apply metallic fabric glue around the beads.

9. Cut 3" strips of the black material, fuse interfacing onto the back, and sew a border around the pillow top.

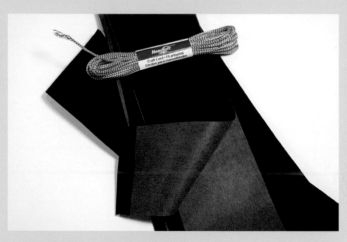

10. Press seams open. Using a pearl foot, cording and invisible thread, couch the cording in the well of the border seams.

11. Couch cording onto the back of the pillow and embroider your signature.

12. Add a light trim on the outside of the pillow. Sew the zipper (see directions on page 45), stuff and the pillow is finished!

HINT: To cut off the back of the shank using a pair of wire clippers, place the button right side down against the palm of your hand with the shank side up. Place the wire cutters on the back of the shank. Turn your hand upside down and snip the shank off. This is a safe way to cut so the shank does not fly in your eye. It also keeps the shank on your cutting table for easier disposal.

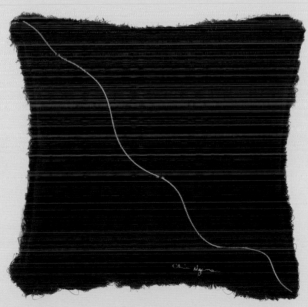

PILLOW BACK

SERENGETI SUNRISE

Material Ideas

- 22" square piece of upholstery fabric for base
- 22" square piece of upholstery fabric for pillow back
- 4" strips of same fabric for pieced borders (8 strips)
- 30" square piece of fusible fleece
- 30" lengths (3" - 4" wide) of 2 separate batiks (2 total)
- 10" square batik for inner circle
- 10" square piece of sheer brown nylon netting
- Decorative yarn
- Gold cording
- Jewel glue
- Copper metallic ribbon thread
- Black metallic ribbon thread
- Invisible thread
- 3 colors of fusible fiber
- Lite Steam-A-Seam
- Button
- Teflon fusing sheet
- Black and gold metallic serger thread for trim
  - Or 3 yd. commercial variegated metallic trim (4" wide)
- Invisible-zipper and narrow straight-stitch foot
- Glue stick
- Fiberfill

I HAVE ALWAYS LOVED AFRICAN ART. THE COLORS AND THE DESIGNS ARE SO RICH WITH THE PASSION OF THE NATIVE CULTURES. THERE IS ALSO SOMETHING ABOUT THE ANIMAL-PRINT MATERIALS THAT IS EXOTIC AND FREE-SPIRITED.

I REALLY WANTED TO CREATE SOMETHING THAT SPOKE OF AFRICA. THIS PILLOW CAME TO ME WHEN I ENVISIONED THE ALLURE OF A TIGER'S EYE. NOT TO MENTION MY CAT JUMPED UP ON MY SEWING TABLE AND LOOKED AT ME WITH HER MAGNIFICENT EYES, WAITING FOR ME TO SCOLD HER!

1. Cut a 22" square of upholstery fabric for the base material.

2. Fuse Lite Steam-A-Seam to the back of batik fabric. Fold the batik fabric in half, and cut a 10" circle of the batik using a circle-cutter tool. Unfold the circle. Remove the paper backing from the Lite Steam-A-Seam.

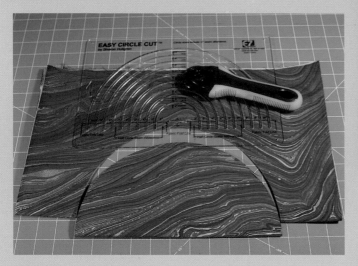

3. Fold the circle in four quarters to find the center.

4. Match the center of the circle to the center of the square. Fuse the circle to the base fabric following the Steam-A-Seam instructions.

5. Cut a piece of sheer brown nylon netting large enough to fit over the circle. Use a fusible spray adhesive to tack it down.

6. Trim off the excess netting around the circle.

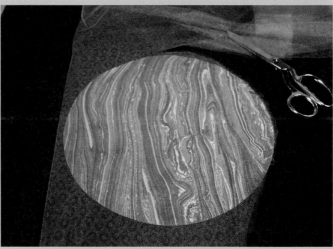

HINT: BE SURE TO USE LITE STEAM-A-SEAM. ANYTHING HEAVIER WILL GUM UP YOUR NEEDLE OR CAUSE THREAD TO BREAK.

7. Stipple on the circle with a flat metallic ribbon thread and a free-motion foot.

9. Use black flat metallic thread to create the free-motion stitches radiating out to the edge of the circle all the way around. This will also help hold the fusible fiber better.

8. Place three different colors of fusible fiber onto the circle in a random fashion. Fuse them together using a Teflon sheet over the circle.

10. Cut 3" strips of two colors of satin fabrics.

11. Punch the strips around the circle.

12. Using a Miraclestitcher (or a pearl foot) and invisible thread, couch yarn in the seams of the outer circles.

13. Cut four strips of upholstery fabric approximately 4" wide. Sew them around the pillow top. Press the seams open.

14. Using a pearl foot and invisible thread, couch yarn with a narrow zig-zag stitch in the seams where you just sewed the strips.

15. Using a copper-colored flat metallic thread, stitch a row of decorative stitches inside the center circle. You can use satin stitches or a stitch of your choice.

16. Using a variegated metallic thread, free-motion stipple inside the two outer circle bands.

17. Use a pearl foot to couch cording to the band-edge of the outer circle. If you wish, you can make your own cording with gold metallic serger thread and a cording maker (I used one from Bond of America).

18. Cut a piece of fusible fleece to the size of the pillow top, and apply it on the back of the pillow top. The fleece gives the center of the pillow a raised look.

19. Free-motion stipple with black metallic thread. Do not stipple inside the circle or you will lose the raised effect.

☀ HINT: IF YOU DON'T HAVE A FRINGE MAKER OR ARE SHORT ON TIME, CONSIDER USING A PRE-MADE COMMERCIAL TRIM.

20. Use black and gold metallic serger thread and yarn to make trim. Wrap the yarn and thread around your trim maker. Remove the fringe from the device, keeping the metal bars within the fringe. Put the attachment under the sewing machine and sew a seam next to the right side of the metal bar. Stitch over this several times to hold all the layers of yarn and thread together.

21. Apply the trim.

22. Make fringe from the same material as the trim and apply to the center of the pillow. Glue a button on the center of the pillow.

23. Add a back to the pillow. Add an invisible-zipper with a narrow straight-stitch foot and the technique shown on pages 53 and 71.

PILLOW BACK

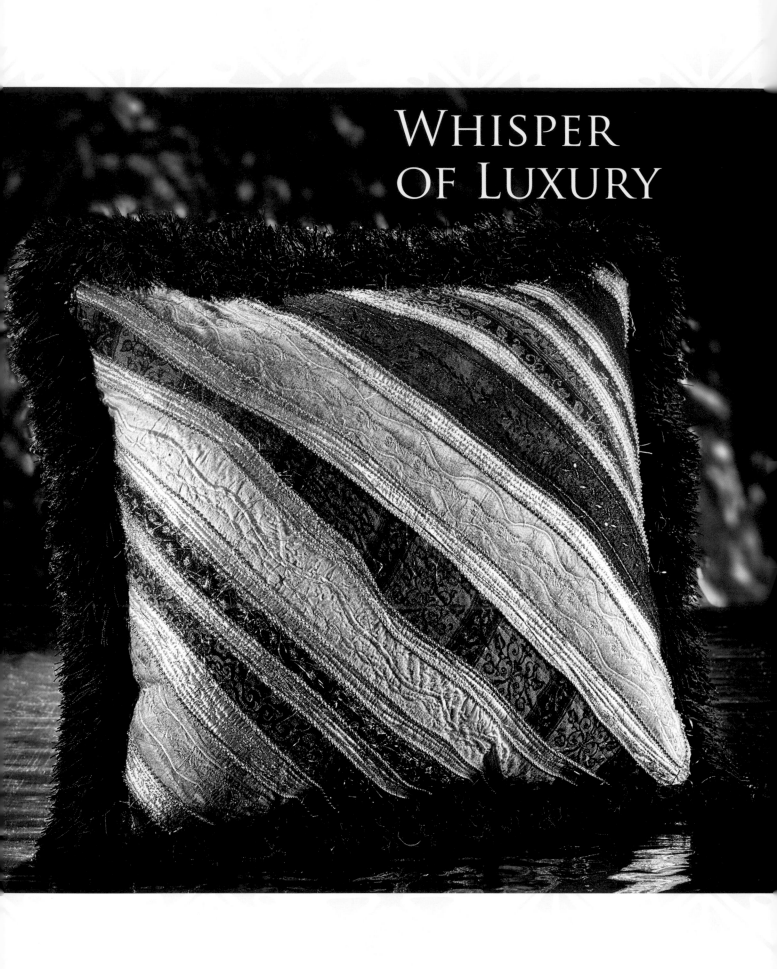

WHISPER OF LUXURY

MATERIAL IDEAS

* 20" square duck cloth for base
* 20" square medium-weight upholstery fabric for pillow back
* 1/8 yd. each, five colors of satin
* 1/4 yd. gold lamé
* Fusible interfacing
* Gold rayon thread
* Tan rayon thread
* Black metallic thread
* Gold metallic thread
* Invisible thread
* 10 yd. pearl strand
* 2 1/2 yd. heavy commercial trim (2" wide)
* Invisible zipper and narrow straight-stitch foot
* Glue stick
* Fiberfill

FOR THIS NEXT PILLOW, I WANTED A FEELING OF ELEGANCE. TO ACHIEVE THIS EFFECT, I USED A PUNCHING TECHNIQUE CALLED STRIP PIECING WITH SATIN IN BLACK, TAN AND A PRINT ALTERNATING WITH STRIPS OF GOLD LAMÉ.

SOME OF THE FABRICS I USED HAD PAINTED SEQUINS IN THEM. THE BLACK FABRIC HAD A PLASTIC SEQUIN GLUED ON, WHICH CAUGHT MY NEEDLES. IF YOU WANT SEQUINS ON YOUR PILLOW, ADD THEM AFTER THE PILLOW IS FINISHED.

1. Cut a 20" square base fabric.

2. Cut at least three colors of satin into strips of varying widths and lay them diagonally on the base fabric. Alternate the fabrics. Begin punching the strips down, overlapping each strip on the next when punching. Cover the entire pillow top. Be sure to punch the fabric firmly.

3. When the strips of satin you have punched down cover the whole pillow top, punch 2"-wide strips of gold lamé on top of the satin seam lines. You will get some fraying but don't be tempted to cut the threads. Fraying adds a look of elegance. You may double up the strips of lamé when punching to add some extra meat.

4. Apply fusible interfacing to the back of the pillow top.

5. Sew decorative stitches onto the punched satin strips with two colors of rayon thread and a black metallic thread. You decide what stitches you want to use. I used satin stitches, a leaf stitch and other stitches randomly.

6. Stitch straight rows onto the gold lamé with a gold metallic thread.

7. Zig-zag stitch 2-mm craft pearls along the edge of each strip of lamé using invisible thread and a pearl foot.

8. Sew on a heavy, dense home décor fringe trim.

9. Because the trim is quite thick, you cannot use an invisible-zipper foot to sew the invisible zipper on. You will need to use a narrow straight-stitch foot.

10. Sew the zipper to the back of the pillow first, keeping a presser-foot distance away from the teeth. This distance allows for a space between the teeth and the pillow fringe and makes it easier to zip the pillow shut. The width from the edge of the pillow will vary based on the trim's seam width. On this pillow, the distance from the edge of the material to the zipper is ½".

PILLOW BACK

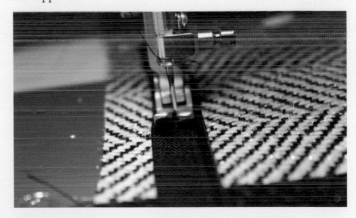

11. Finish the pillow, stuff, sit back and smile!

SANDS OF SAHARA

MATERIAL IDEAS

* 18" square heavy gold satin
* 18" square heavy cream satin for back
* 4" strips hand-dyed textured fabric for borders
* 4" strips light gold fabric for back borders
* Variegated metallic ribbon thread
* Invisible thread
* Fusible fiber
* Decorative yarn or cording
* Crystals
* Gold metallic fabric paint
* Silver metallic fabric paint
* 2½ yd. commercial braided trim (9" wide)
* Invisible zipper and narrow straight-stitch foot
* Glue stick
* Fiberfill

SWAROVSKI CRYSTALS, FUSIBLE FIBERS, METALLIC THREADS—A FIBER CONSTRUCTION ARTIST'S CANDY STORE!

AS I WAS WALKING THROUGH THE FABRIC STORE, I STUMBLED ACROSS A NEW LINE OF FABRIC CONSISTING OF BEAUTIFULLY GRADATED SATINS IN A LOVELY TEXTURE. THE ONE I CHOSE IS CALLED THE PROM COLLECTION. I CAME HOME AND LOOKED AT IT ON MY PRESSING TABLE—IT JUST SCREAMED STAR BURST!

THIS PILLOW IS TRULY ELEGANT. IN PERSON, WHEN THE LIGHT HITS IT FROM DIFFERENT ANGLES, IT SPARKLES AND GLISTENS! THOUGH THE COLORS COME TOGETHER TO AN ALMOST MONOCHROMATIC HUE, ITS BALANCE IS TRULY OUTSTANDING!

1. Cut an 18" square of heavy satin material for the base fabric. Fuse interfacing onto the back. Please be sure your iron steams and doesn't drip. Drips can cause water marks that show on the satin.

2. Spread fusible fiber across the pillow top.

3. Press a Teflon sheet with a dry iron for several seconds across the whole pillow top. Let it cool, then remove the Teflon pressing sheet while holding the fusible fiber down against the pillow top.

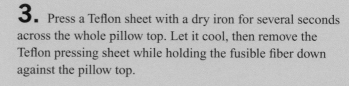

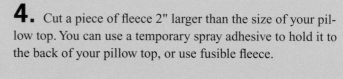

4. Cut a piece of fleece 2" larger than the size of your pillow top. You can use a temporary spray adhesive to hold it to the back of your pillow top, or use fusible fleece.

5. Attach a free-motion foot to your machine, and drop your feed dogs. Starting in one corner of the pillow, stitch straight, radiating lines in a fan pattern across the rest of the pillow over the fusible fiber.

6. Overlap and stitch these lines many times until you are satisfied with the amount of thread and the fusible fiber is firmly sewn down.

7. Apply beads using metallic paint.

8. Apply Swarovski crystals with a hot-fix applicator.

9. Cut four 3" strips of a coordinating textured fabric and fuse interfacing onto the back. (You can fuse interfacing onto the whole fabric first then cut your strips, if you wish.)

10. Before applying the strips to the pillow top, randomly stitch on top of the strips with a variegated metallic thread that coordinates with the fabric and your outside trim.

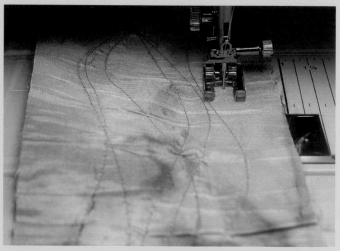

11. Sew the strips around the pillow top. Sew the left side first, then the right side. Press open, then trim to match the pillow top. Sew the top strip and the bottom strip along the whole width of the pillow. Press open and trim.

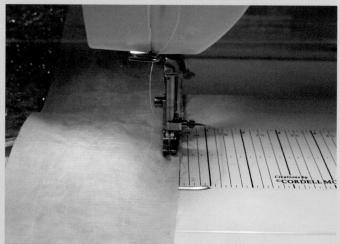

12. Use a pearl foot and invisible thread to attach cording.

13. Sew on an upholstery trim beginning on the left edge of the pillow.

14. Apply gold metallic paint randomly across the pillow top and smear it to give it more character.

15. Choose a fabric for the back of the pillow, apply gold metallic paint, beads and cording, as in Step 12.

16. Attach an invisible zipper with a narrow straight-stitch foot, and stuff the pillow.

PILLOW BACK

PETALS ON THE NILE

MATERIAL IDEAS

* 18" x 12" black doeskin or cotton velveteen fabric
* 18" x 12" fabric for pillow back
* 5 colors of thread including black
* Thread scraps
* Invisible thread
* Opal-colored metallic thread
* Fusible fiber
* Crystals
* Craft glue
* 1³/₄ yd. lightweight trim (4" wide)
* Invisible zipper and invisible-zipper foot
* Glue stick
* Fiberfill

SOMETIMES, I SIT AND SEW DIFFERENT DECORATIVE STITCHES ON MY SEWING MACHINES FOR HOURS ON END. IT RELAXES ME, AND IT ALLOWS ME TO TEST MANY OF THE HUNDREDS OF BUILT-IN STITCHES I HAVE.

WHENEVER I SEW, I KEEP A JAR FOR ALL MY CUT THREADS. THE JAR IS FULL OF METALLICS, RAYONS, CONSTRUCTION THREADS AND EVEN METALLIC SERGER THREADS. I HAVE SEEN PEOPLE CREATE "THREAD FABRIC" BY SANDWICHING THREADS BETWEEN TWO LAYERS OF WATER-SOLUBLE STABILIZER, SEWING MANY ROWS ACROSS THE STABILIZER, AND THEN RINSING THE STABILIZER AWAY.

FOR THIS PILLOW, I WANTED TO TRY SOMETHING LIKE A THREAD FABRIC WHILE PLAYING WITH ALL OF THOSE WONDERFUL DECORATIVE STITCHES. BUT I KNEW THAT THREADS ALONE WOULD NOT BE ENOUGH GLITZ FOR ME, SO I REACHED FOR MY ANGELINA.

1. Cut an 18" x 12" piece of doeskin material. Fuse interfacing onto the back.

2. Lay the fabric right side up on your pressing table, and randomly spread cut threads over the pillow top.

4. Cover the pillow top with a Teflon sheet and press with a dry iron. Let the Teflon cool, then peel it away while holding down the thread and fiber. You'll be amazed when you see that the fused fiber has bonded around the thread, creating a new piece of fabric! Apply another layer of fusible fiber and fuse. No threads should be hanging out of the Angelina.

3. Spread four different colors of fusible fiber over the threads. Do not be stingy with the fiber. Mix everything together like cake batter.

5. Apply a fusible spray to adhere the thread fabric to the black base material so it will hold in place for decorative stitching.

6. To select threads for decorative stitching, lay out different spools to see which colors will coordinate with the thread fabric as shown.

7. Use an embroidery foot or satin stitch foot to stitch a row of decorative satin stitches as shown.

8. Apply more rows of decorative stitching. I changed the stitches as I sewed, but all my stitches were variations of a decorative satin stitch.

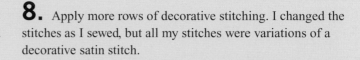

9. After all the stitching is complete, lay out fusible fiber onto a Teflon pressing sheet. After laying out the fiber, cover the fiber with the other half of the Teflon pressing sheet, and press. Apply more fusible fiber and repeat so the new fabric is firm and has some beef to it.

10. Cut flower petals from the fiber, using your eye as a guide. Cut as many petals as you wish for your flower blooms. I cut four to six petals for each flower.

12. Next, change to a free-motion foot. Using an opal-colored metallic thread, sew continuously in a circle to form the center of each flower. Sew over and over until the thread builds up and becomes hard.

11. Put an open-toe foot or free-motion foot onto your machine and drop your feed dogs. Set your machine to a medium zig-zag stitch, and tack the leaves down in a random fashion using invisible thread.

13. Apply a Swarovski crystal with a hot-fix applicator to each of the four flower centers.

14. Using your serger, serge the four edges around the pillow. Or use an over-lock foot and over-lock stitch on your conventional machine to finish the edges.

15. Apply trim of your choice around the outside of the pillow.

16. Attach the zipper, sew the pillow closed, turn it right side out, and stuff.

PILLOW BACK

MATERIAL IDEAS

* 13" x 20" duck cloth for base
* 13" x 20" fabric for pillow back
* $1/3$ yd. purple satin
* $1/4$ yd. black fabric for squares and side borders
* Fusible interfacing
* Gold metallic thread
* Black metallic thread
* Black metallic serger thread
* Invisible thread
* Crystals
* Craft glue
* Craft mirrors
* Opal-colored metallic fabric paint
* $3^1/4$ yd. black and white striped cording
* 2 yd. commercial trim
* Lite Steam-A-Seam
* Invisible zipper and narrow straight-stitch foot
* Glue stick
* Fiberfill

I FOUND THE INSPIRATION FOR THIS PILLOW WHEN LOOKING THROUGH A BOOK I HAD ON THE MYTHOLOGY OF EGYPT. RA IS THE EGYPTIAN SUN GOD, AND HIS NAME CAN BE TRANSLATED TO MEAN "CREATIVE POWER!"

THE ART FROM EXOTIC LANDS IS BEAUTIFUL AND INSPIRING, ESPECIALLY ART FROM EGYPT WITH ITS MODERNISTIC GEOMETRIC DESIGNS. ONE OF THE BEST THINGS I LEARNED IS HOW TO MAKE SATIN LOOK LIKE SUEDE UNDER THE PUNCHING MACHINE.

1. Cut a 20" x 13" piece of duck cloth for the base material. As always, you can cut your base fabric any size you would like.

2. Cut 3" or 4" pieces of purple satin. Punch the satin down the center of the base material, working your way out to the edges of the pillow. Overlap each piece as you lay them down to punch. Be sure your punching is firm and covers the pieces of satin entirely. As you punch, the satin will take on the look of suede. Be sure to blend the edges well.

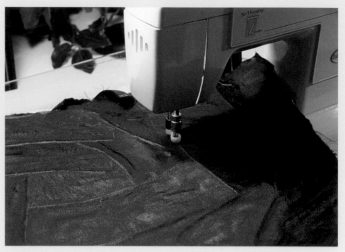

3. Cut six 4" x 4" squares of black satin. Lay them out in two rows as seen in the photo. Pin each square in place. Do not use a fusible spray, as this will distort the fabric during punching.

4. Punch the squares to the pillow top. Remember to remove each pin before you get near it when punching. Don't worry if the squares shift slightly, it adds artistic character.

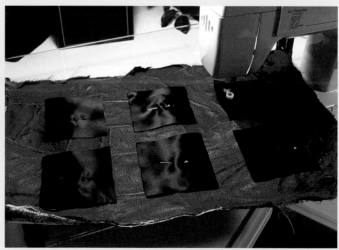

5. Cut several strips of gold lamé fabric with a rotary cutter as shown.

6. Lay the lamé down onto the center of each square like confetti, and punch it down. Layer and build up the lamé by punching a strip with a few punches, then punching another strip directly on top. You may double- or even triple-layer each strip of lamé. The lamé will fray, but don't worry, this adds texture and later will be secured with top stitching.

7. Fuse interfacing onto the back of the pillow top.

8. Set your machine up for free-motion sewing with gold metallic thread and a top-stitch needle. Set your tension to 1.8. Sew random circles on the lamé. Sew enough to reinforce the lamé onto the base fabric while giving it a nice, circular design.

9. Put on a cording foot, raise your feed dogs and set your machine up for a decorative domino stitch. Experiment with the width, length and tension. All machines vary, so test before you sew on your pillow.

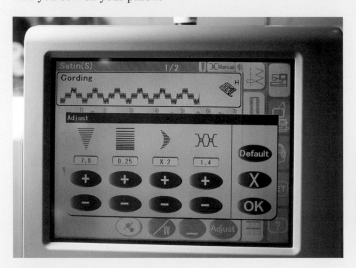

10. Couch down three strands of black metallic serger thread with the domino stitch and black metallic thread. Sew intersecting rows across the whole pillow.

11. Next, attach an appliqué foot and set your machine for an appliqué stitch. Using invisible thread, stitch around the black squares.

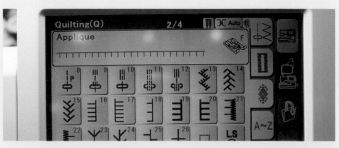

12. Attach an open-toe embroidery foot. Set your machine for a decorative stitch (I chose a Greek stitch). Using black metallic thread, stitch four rows along the outside perimeter and two rows each across the width of the pillow between the three sections of black squares.

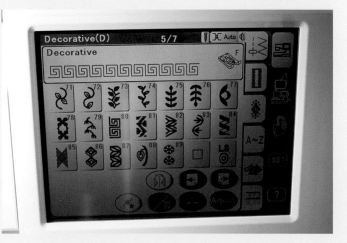

13. Glue mirrors to the center of each lamé starburst.

14. Apply Swarovski crystals with hot-fix applicator.

15. Apply crystal, opal-colored metallic fabric paint around each of the mirrors.

16. For borders, fuse interfacing onto the back of $^{1}/_{2}$ yard of doeskin fabric. Cut the material into four 3" strips.

HINT: USE PLENTY OF STEAM WHEN PRESSING THE STRIPS OPEN. IF DESIRED, USE A PRESS CLOTH TO PREVENT SHINE ON THE FABRIC.

17. Sew a strip to the left side of the pillow. Press the panel open, using plenty of steam. Sew a strip to the right side of the fabric. Press the panel open. Repeat for the top and bottom.

18. Fuse Steam-A-Seam double-sided webbing to the back of a black-and-white-striped braided trim.

19. Place the trim over the seam lines of the black and purple fabric starting on the left and right sides. Peel the paper off the Steam-A-Seam, and fuse the braid in place.

20. Repeat for the top and bottom but extend the braid to the ends of the pillow.

21. Attach an open-toe embroidery foot. Using a straight stitch and invisible thread, sew down the black rows of the trim.

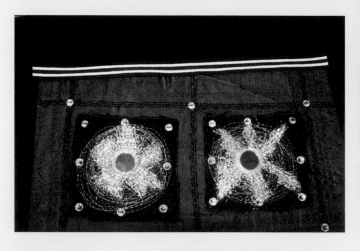

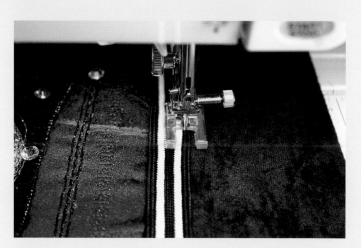

22. Add a heavy, rope-braid trim.

23. Detail the back of the pillow. Add the zipper using the narrow straight-stitch foot (as shown on pages 53 and 71) and stuff with fiberfill.

PILLOW BACK

Material Ideas

* 18" square duck cloth for base
* 18" square fabric for pillow back
* $^1/_4$ yd. lamé (42" wide)
* $^1/_4$ yd. total of 3 to 5 colors of batik
* Chenille yarn
* Flat ribbon yarn
* Gold metallic thread
* Invisible thread
* Craft mirrors
* Craft glue
* Gold metallic fabric paint
* Opalescent metallic fabric paint
* Tulip fabric paint
* $2^1/_4$ yd. lightweight trim ($1^3/_4$" wide)
* $2^1/_4$ yd. beaded trim ($1^1/_2$" wide)
* Invisible zipper and invisible-zipper foot
* Glue stick
* Fiberfill

PEOPLE TODAY LOVE BEADS AND BRIGHT, SHINY FABRICS. THIS PILLOW WAS INSPIRED BY THE DECORATIVE IDEAS OF INDIA AND BY CRAZY QUILTING. IT INCORPORATES CRAZY PIECING, LAMÉ INSERTING, YARN FLOWERS, BEADS AND METALLIC FRINGE. HERE IS A PILLOW MADE ON THE TRADITIONAL SEWING MACHINE WITH A MIRACLESTITCHER OR PEARL FOOT FOR THE YARN EMBELLISHMENTS.

1. Cut a 16" square piece of duck cloth.

2. Cut a triangle of hand-dyed fabric from a 4" square.

3. Lay the triangle in the center of the duck cloth.

4. Fuse interfacing to the back of your piece of lamé. Please use a low heat iron and no steam. Steam will cause the lamé to distort.

5. Cut 2" strips of lamé the width of the fabric so you have nice long strips to work with. Fold the strips in half length-wise. Now you have 1" doubled strips of lamé.

6. Cut your batik fabrics into 3" strips.

7. Lay a folded strip of lamé on one side of the triangle and pin. Lay the 3" strip of fabric on top of the folded lamé and pin. Stitch the fabric and lamé down with a ¼" seam along one side of the triangle. You may use any color thread because it will not show.

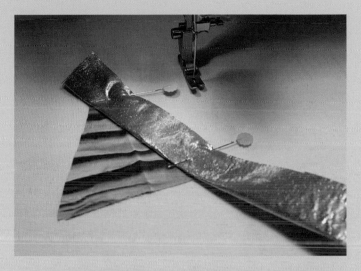

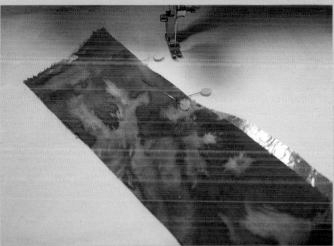

8. After sewing the seam down one side of the triangle, fold the fabric and lamé open and press flat. Then cut off the extra tails of fabric that extend beyond the triangle.

10. Continue adding strips of lamé and fabric around your pillow, turning clockwise as you overlap each new addition.

9. Repeat Steps 7 and 8 on the opposite side of the triangle as shown.

12. Attach a Miraclestitcher or pearl foot, and thread your machine with invisible thread. Drop your feed dogs. Couch down green chenille yarn to make free-motion flowers and leaves around the pillow. (I used a stitch width of 1.5.)

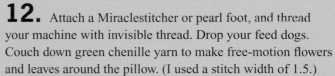

11. Attach a braiding foot to your machine, and set it up for a couching stitch with gold metallic thread. Couch down a decorative ribbon yarn with the gold metallic thread, moving around the pillow in large curves in a random fashion.

13. Glue craft mirrors to the center of each yarn flower. Apply metallic fabric paints to make decorative, free-form designs on the pillow.

14. After the paint dries, add beaded trim around the pillow top with a narrow straight foot as shown.

15. Over the beaded trim, add a light, metallic trim so the pillow has a double layer of trim.

16. Cut a piece of heavyweight cotton for the backing fabric. It can be hand-dyed or hand-painted or a solid color, as long as it coordinates with the front. I hand-painted the fabric shown using Tulip paints and textile medium. After paint dries for 48 hours, heat set to be permanent.

17. Next, use a fabric marking pencil and freehand draw a flower design on the backing fabric.

18. Attach your Miraclestitcher or pearl foot. Use the same green chenille yarn to couch over the drawn design.

19. Glue a colored jewel onto the center of the pillow-back flower. Wait for it to dry. Then embroider your name, if you wish.

20. Attach the backing and zipper. Stuff the pillow, and you are done!

PILLOW BACK

OASIS

MATERIAL IDEAS

* 18" square heavy, lime-green satin
* 18" square fabric for pillow back
* 18" square fusible fleece
* Opal-colored flat metallic thread
* Fusible fiber
* Fusible interfacing
* Variegated gold metallic thread
* Jewel glue
* Invisible thread
* 42" beaded costume jewelry
* Craft mirrors
* Crystals
* Craft glue
* $2^1/_2$ yd. heavy trim ($2^1/_4$" wide)
* Invisible zipper and narrow straight-stitch foot
* Glue stick
* Stuffing

THE INSPIRATION FOR THIS PILLOW CAME FROM LOOKING ON MY CUTTING TABLE AT ALL MY FABRICS AND EMBELLISHMENTS. THE MOMENT I PICKED UP THE PALE LIME-GREEN SATIN FABRIC AND THE JEWELS I HAD NEXT TO IT, A RUSH JUST CAME OVER ME. I ENVISIONED A PILLOW THAT HAD A FEELING OF OPAL AND GOLD COLORED ICE ON TOP OF SHERBET. YES, I WAS DIETING AGAIN AND FOOD WAS ON MY MIND. WHEN I FINISHED THIS PILLOW, I WENT TO THE STORE IMMEDIATELY TO FIND SOME LOW-CARB SHERBET!

1. Cut an 18" square of fashion fabric—in this case, I used a heavy, lime green satin. Fuse interfacing onto the back. Don't worry if the satin becomes slightly distorted.

2. Cut an 18" square of fusible fleece, and lightly fuse it to the back of the fabric just to prevent shifting.

3. Set up your sewing machine for free-motion sewing with a free-motion foot. Thread an opal-colored thread. (I used Sulky sliver thread in opal.)

4. Stitch small- to medium-size stippling in a meandering fashion, starting from the center of the fabric and working your way around to the outside edges.

5. Next, spread fusible fiber in two colors randomly across the center of the pillow, and fuse it in place with a pressing sheet. Lightly spray a temporary adhesive to the back of the fusible fiber to hold it to the pillow top.

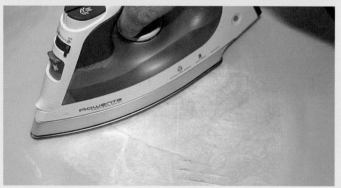

6. Choose a stretch stitch using the default setting on your computer sewing machine. I chose this stitch to give the pillow a little wiggle. Some machines call this a lightning stitch.

8. Starting at the center of the pillow, radiate lines of stretch stitching out toward each corner of the pillow top. The free-motion stitching looks great and helps to secure the fusible fiber to the pillow.

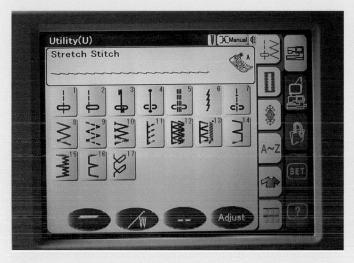

7. Attach a free motion foot and lower your feed dogs. Thread your machine with flat, variegated gold metallic thread (I use Sulky sliver thread). Be sure to test your stitch width before stitching on your pillow.

9. If you choose, you may also do some broomstick bristle stitching at the end of the lines.

10. Find some beaded jewelry, cut it, and lay it out in a cross intersection on the middle of the pillow. If the necklace has a pendant, place it in the center of the pillow. Tack the jewelry down with jewel glue.

11. After the glue dries, transfer the pillow top to your sewing machine. Take the foot off your machine, lower your feed dogs, and thread the machine with invisible thread. Use a medium zig-zag stitch to tack the necklace in place. Be sure your stitches pass over the beads as you tack the necklace in various places.

12. Cut a piece of fabric for the back of the pillow. I used a brown-colored satin the same size as the pillow top. Fuse interfacing to the back of the backing fabric.

13. Select a yarn that complements the pillow colors. Attach a pearl foot and thread your machine with invisible thread. Using a zig-zag stitch, couch the yarn down in a random design.

14. Thread your machine with flat, variegated gold metallic thread. Select a decorative stitch on your machine; I chose a New Sculpture stitch. Using an open-toe or satin-stitch foot, stitch wavy rows over the yarn.

15. Attach a zipper closure as I demonstrated on pages 53 and 71. Sew the front and back of the pillow together. Stuff the pillow, zip it closed and enjoy!

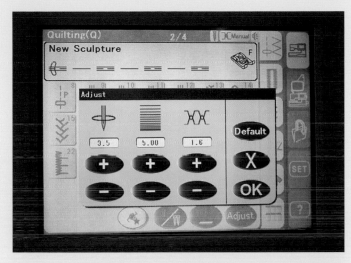

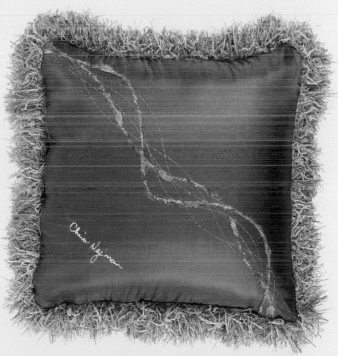

PILLOW BACK

ROMANCE OVER COSTA RICA

MATERIAL IDEAS

* 22" x 16" duck cloth for base
* 22" x 16" fabric for pillow back
* 1/2 yd. light green suede-back satin
* 1/2 yd. dark green suede-back satin
* 1 yd. silk fabric for side strips and backing
* Light-colored fusible fiber
* Dark-colored fusible fiber
* Gold metallic thread

* Black metallic thread
* Invisible thread
* 3 yd. strand of gold pearls (2 mm)
* 2 1/4 yd. braided trim (6" wide)
* Fusible interfacing
* Yarn
* Invisible thread
* Invisible zipper
* Glue stick
* Fiberfill

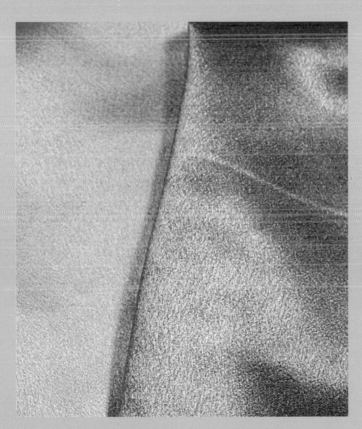

ONE DAY AFTER MY SHOW AIRED ON QNN, I RECEIVED A VERY NICE EMAIL FROM A VIEWER IN THE RAIN FOREST OF COSTA RICA. I IMMEDIATELY WENT TO THE INTERNET TO FIND EXACTLY WHERE THIS VIEWER RESIDED. IN MY SEARCH, I FOUND AERIAL PHOTOS OF JUNGLES AND GREEN RAIN FORESTS DOWN IN CENTRAL AMERICA, AND INSPIRATION STRUCK. HOW COULD I INTERPRET THAT BEAUTY WITH A PILLOW? I SET OUT TO CREATE THREE-DIMENSIONAL TEXTURE, LIKE THE VIEW FROM A PLANE FLYING HIGH ABOVE THE LUSCIOUS GREENS OF A BEAUTIFUL JUNGLE.

1. Start with a 22" x 16" base fabric of duck cloth.

2. Cut several 3" or 4" strips of two colors of suede-back satin. The tightness of your punching may cause the amount of fabric you need to vary. For average punching tightness, you will need ¼ yd. to ½ yd. of each color.

3. Begin to punch the first color of satin down. Scrunch the fabric together and leave some fabric out when punching, as shown in the photo. Be sure to overlap the fabric and punch the edges well.

4. Punch down the second color of fabric. When I originally created this pillow, I envisioned lush, green land with darker hillsides and valleys. I bridged my two shades together in places so I didn't get a striped look.

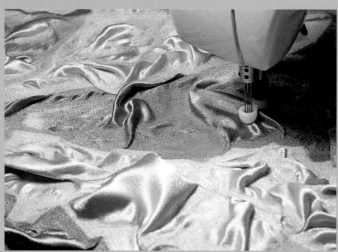

5. Punch small pieces of fusible fiber down in different areas of the pillow. I blended two different colors for the most dramatic effect.

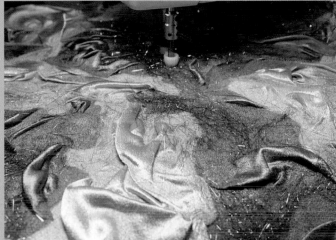

6. After punching the fibers, place the pillow top on your ironing board. Hold the iron about 2" from the pillow top, and hit the steam button to help fuse the fusible fiber to itself.

7. Set your sewing machine up for free-motion scribbling. Scribble across the pillow with gold metallic thread. Be careful not to scribble down all your wonderful texture. Scribble black metallic thread to add contrast in certain areas within the landscape.

8. Using a pearl foot and invisible thread, couch down 2-mm craft pearls with a medium zig-zag stitch.

10. Fuse interfacing onto the back of a piece of hand-painted silk fabric (I used silk dyed by Lady Dye Fabrics). Cut the fabric into four 2½" strips.

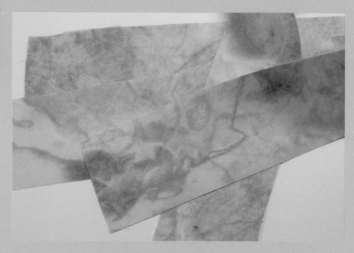

9. If you want to add more black detail to the pillow like I did, free-motion stitch more lines with black metallic ribbon thread.

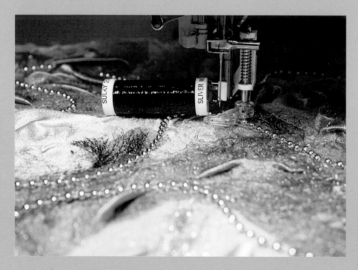

11. Sew the strips around the perimeter of the pillow, stopping ¼" from each edge to leave room for the mitered corners. The fabric will hang in the wind ¼" from each corner.

12. Press the seams open.

13. At each corner of the pillow top, fold the un-sewn parts of the strips onto each other. Following the edge of the folded pillow, mark a 45-degree line.

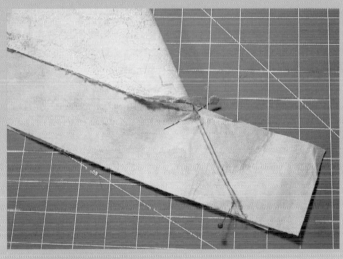

14. Because you originally stopped ¼" from each edge, begin sewing on the edge of the pillow top down the 45-degree line on the strips that you marked.

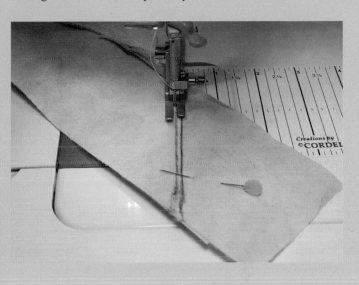

15. Press the seams open and you have a perfectly mitered corner. Do this on all four corners.

16. Trim the excess fabric off in the back, leaving a 1/4" seam allowance.

17. Select a piece of coordinating fabric for the back of the pillow. Fuse interfacing to the back of it.

HINT: WHEN I MADE THE BACK OF THIS PILLOW, I DID NOT HAVE A FULL PIECE OF THE SILK FABRIC, BUT I HAD ENOUGH SCRAPS TO PIECE A BACK TOGETHER. AFTER SEWING THE PIECES TOGETHER, I FUSED INTERFACING ONTO THE BACK OF IT.

18. Attach a pearl foot or a Miraclestitcher, and thread your machine with invisible thread.

19. Using the free-motion couching technique, couch down yarn in a random design. (I used variegated green yarn because it complemented the rest of the pillow.) Be sure to follow the instructions that come with your pearl foot or Miraclestitcher. The zig-zag should be 1.5 mm, and your feed dogs should be lowered. It is much like free-motion embroidcry—a slow and smooth motion.

20. Add an upholstery trim and a zipper closure. Finish the construction, stuff the pillow, and you're ready to start your next pillow!

PILLOW BACK

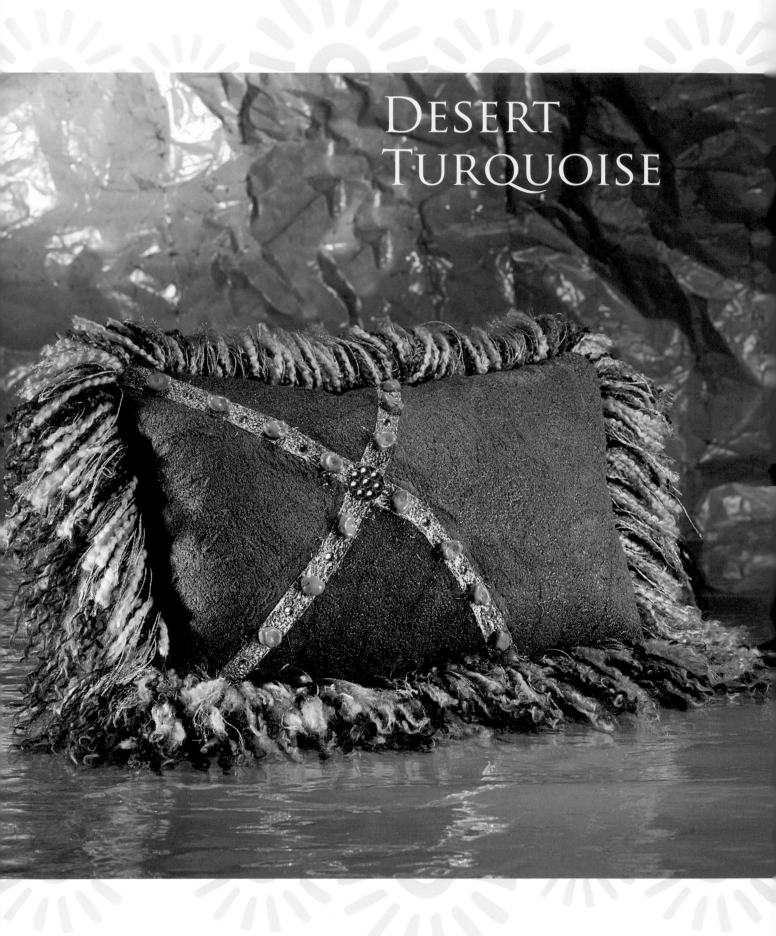

DESERT
TURQUOISE

MATERIAL IDEAS

* 20" x 13" duck cloth for base
* 20" x 13" fabric for pillow back
* ⅛ yd. suede-back satin in light turquoise
* ⅛ yd. suede-back satin in dark turquoise
* 1 yd. silver lamé
* Fusible interfacing
* Silver metallic thread
* Coordinating rayon thread
* Marking Tool
* Jewel glue

* Silver metallic ribbon thread
* Turquoise necklace (or stones or beads)
* 3 spools serger thread and yarn for trim (3" - 4½" wide)
  * Or 2 yd. commercial trim
* Crystals
* 1 craft mirror
* Invisible zipper and narrow straight-stitch foot
* Glue stick
* Fiberfill

ONE DAY I WAS LOOKING AT A NECKLACE MY FRIEND WAS WEARING. THE CENTER OF THE NECKLACE WAS A BROOCH MADE FROM TURQUOISE WITH RUNNING RHINESTONES. I REALLY LIKED THE TEXTURE AND DESIGN. I THOUGHT ABOUT HOW I COULD MAKE A PILLOW INSPIRED BY HER NECKLACE. I WANTED TO HAVE THE PILLOW LOOK LIKE THE TEXTURE OF STONE. HERE'S HOW TO DO IT.

1. Cut a 20" x 13" piece of duck cloth for your base fabric.

2. Draw a curved line on the cloth as shown. Use a permanent marker or pencil.

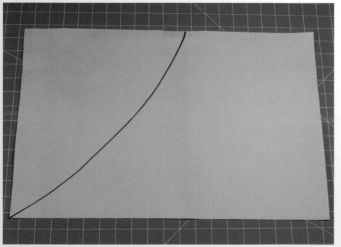

3. Draw your second line—it should cross over the first.

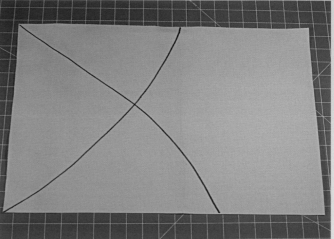

4. Cut one piece of suede-back satin into small pieces. Punch the pieces to the base fabric in one section of the pillow, overlapping each piece as you punch. Notice how the texture of the fabric begins to change.

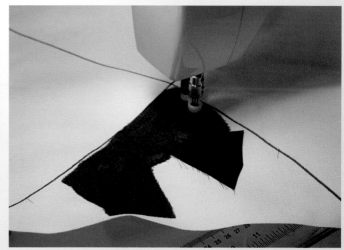

5. Repeat Step 4 on the opposite side.

6. Using the second shade of suede-back satin, repeat Step 4 in the other two sections of the pillow top.

7. Cut eight strips of silver lamé 2" wide. Fold the strips in half lengthwise. Lay a strip across the seams where the suede back satins meet, and punch it down. It will fray a little, but don't worry, that adds to the texture. Don't be tempted to cut the frays off!

8. After punching the lamé strips across all the seams, punch another folded layer as shown.

9. After punching all the fabric down, fuse interfacing to the back of the pillow top.

10. Attach a free-motion embroidery foot to your machine. Start with the silver metallic thread, and scribble over the silver lamé.

11. Next, scribble with the rayon threads over the rest of the pillow top. Do not be afraid to saturate the pillow top with the rayon thread. Remember, scribbling is crossing the lines over and over. As you build up the thread, it will start to feel hard. This is what you want for the stone effect.

12. After scribbling with the rayon thread, scribble with the flat metallic ribbon thread.

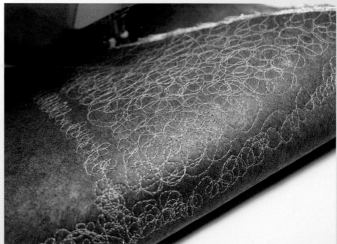

A "BEHIND-THE-SCENES" LOOK AFTER SCRIBBLING.

13. Cut the turquoise necklace, and glue the stones to the pillow along the path of the lamé strips. Glue a craft mirror in the center of the lamé crossings.

14. Attach Swarovski crystals with a hot-fix applicator onto the lamé and onto the mirror.

15. While waiting for the jewel glue to dry, make your fringe with a total of three spools of serger thread (I used YLI Candlelight), yarn and a fringe-making tool.

16. Wrap the three strands of serger thread and yarn around the fringe maker. Remove the unit from the stand, and place it under your sewing machine. Stitch a presser-foot distance away from the edge of the rod as shown in the photo.

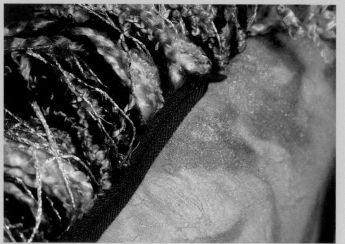

17. Stitch several times up and down this row to ensure the yarn and threads are all stitched together. Remove the fringe, and repeat the whole procedure until you have enough fringe to wrap around the pillow top.

18. Sew the trim to the pillow top, and add an invisible zipper. Because of the bulk of the fringe, you cannot sew the invisible zipper in close to the teeth. Use a narrow ¼" straight-stitch foot.

HERE IS HOW THE ZIPPER WILL LOOK WHEN IT IS FINISHED AND CLOSED. REMEMBER, THIS CONSTRUCTION METHOD IS DONE BECAUSE OF THE BULK OF THE FRINGE. IT IS MUCH BETTER THAN TRYING TO TOP STITCH THE PILLOW CLOSED.

19. Complete the construction of your pillow, stuff it, and you are finished!

PILLOW BACK

MATERIAL IDEAS

* 16" square duck cloth for base
* 16" square fabric for pillow back
* 4" strips of 7-10 varied fabrics including gold lamé
* Metallic ribbon thread in various colors
* 1½ - 1¾ yd. variegated pearls
* Jewel glue
* Craft mirrors

* Invisible thread
* Metallic serger thread in several colors
* 2 yd. trim (2¾" wide)
* ⅛ yd. variegated nylon scarf material
* 1 crystal
* Invisible zipper and invisible-zipper foot
* Glue stick
* Fiberfill

I CREATED THIS DESIGN AFTER WATCHING SATELLITE IMAGES OF A HURRICANE HERE IN FLORIDA WHERE I LIVE. IT IS SO HARD TO BELIEVE THAT SUCH DISASTER COULD HAVE SUCH BEAUTY VIEWING IT FROM ABOVE THE EARTH. THE SWIRL OF THE HURRICANE INTRIGUED ME IN SUCH A WAY THAT I TOOK THE IDEA AND MADE IT MY BASE DESIGN.

1. Cut a 16" square of duck cloth, and draw a circular design with a permanent marker as shown in the photo.

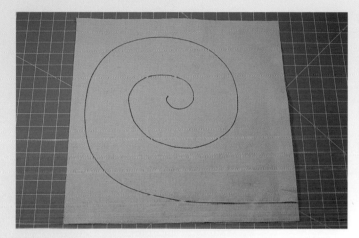

2. Lay out seven 3" or 4" strips of variegated metallic satin fabric that balance nicely together. The strips should be the length of the fabric.

3. Starting at the center of the swirl, begin punching down a strip of fabric along the line.

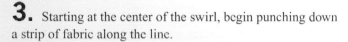

4. If your strip of fabric has two beautiful sides to it, twist it every few inches to give it texture and a different tonal value.

5. Select a complementary strip of fabric, and begin punching it down next to the first strip. Be sure to slightly overlap the strips, and punch the edges well.

6. Continue adding different fabrics next to each other, building an echo effect around the swirl.

7. When punching down the gold lamé, crunch and fold it over to give it more beef and a dynamic texture. If you punch a single layer of lamé down it will fray—we don't want fraying on this pillow.

8. Audition several spools of metallic ribbon thread in various colors to coordinate with the pillow top for free-motion stitching. Attach a free-motion foot to your machine, and lower your feed dogs. Test your tension balance—I usually set mine to 1.8.

9. Use free-motion straight stitches to follow the lines of the different fabrics. Overlap the stitches as you move the fabric back and forth under the free-motion foot. You can use tone-on-tone threads or any coordinating color that matches the color scheme of the fabric.

10. Now, it is time for more dimension! Go into your embellishment stash and find some purple variegated pearls. Attach a pearl foot to your machine.

11. Starting in the center and working along the circular design, use a zig-zag stitch with invisible thread to sew the pearls in place.

12. Now it is time to make a fireworks center fringe. Select several spools of metallic serger thread.

13. Take all the thread into one hand and pull out about five feet. Fold the strands to about a 4" bunch. Lay the threads under the presser foot, and use invisible thread and a straight stitch to tack them down in the center of the pillow top.

14. Make another grouping of these threads, and place them over the first grouping to form a cross. Sew the second grouping down the same way.

15. Cut the ends of the threads, and spread them out. Now you have your fireworks fringe!

16. Tack down a variegated nylon scarf material at a forty five degree angle at each corner of the pillow.

17. To finish the embellishments, glue a crystal in the center of the fireworks fringe using jewel glue. Place craft mirrors randomly on the pillow, and glue them down with gold metallic fabric paint.

18. To help the fireworks fringe lay flat when the pillow stands up, lift the fringe up, and glue several strands down to the base of the pillow.

19. Choose a fringe trim for the outside of the pillow. Use an invisible zipper for the closure.

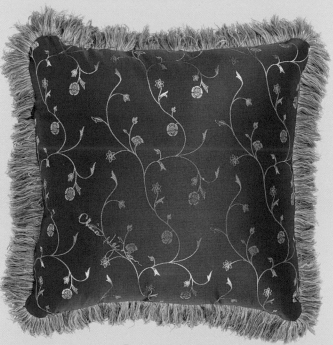

PILLOW BACK

ABOUT THE AUTHOR

Designer and teacher Christopher Nejman has recently appeared on "Sewing with Nancy," Quilt Central TV and Quilter's News Network, in addition to launching his own program on the forthcoming Internet channel, QuiltersTV. Christopher has inspired thousands of sewers around the world with his television appearances, his active teaching schedule and his amazing Web sites.

A native of Pennsylvania, Christopher currently makes his home in Florida. In addition to being a fiber construction artist and teacher, Christopher is a web site designer, photographer, hair stylist and makeup artist. He dreams of bringing elegance and extravagance to the sewing world with a complete sewing-industry makeover!

Christopher's work has appeared in advertisements and instructional material for Brother. For more information, please visit www.christophernejman.com, he loves to hear from fans!

Christopher and the crew of "Sewing with Nancy"

RESOURCES

NOTIONS

EMBELLISHMENT VILLAGE
Angelina
http://embellishmentvillage.com

BOND OF AMERICA
Cording Machine
http://bond-america.com

THE CROWNING TOUCH
Tube Turner
http://www.crowning-touch.com

DELTA JEWEL GLUE
http://www.deltacrafts.com

UNIEK
Crafter's Cording
http://www.uniekinc.com/cord.html

DUNCAN ENTERPRISE
Tulip Paint
http://www.duncancrafts.com/

KANDI CORP
Hot-Fix Crystals
http://www.kandicorp.com/index.htm

PRYM CONSUMER USA
http://www.dritz.com

JUNE TAILOR
http://www.junetailor.com/

DREAM WORLD
Acrylic Extension Tables
http://www.dreamworld-inc.com

JT TRADING
Spray Adhesive
http://www.sprayandfix.com

EZ QUILTING
Marking Tools
http://www.ezquilt.com

MUNDIAL SCISSORS
http://www.mundialusa.com

SCHMETZ NEEDLES
http://www.schmetz.com

BLUE FEATHER
Bobbin Rings, Magnetic Pin Cushion and Caddy
http://www.blue-feather.com

NANCY'S NOTIONS
Fringe Maker
https://www.nancysnotions.com

SCS USA
Klasse Needles
Madeira Threads
info@scsusa1.com

COATS
Zippers and Threads
http://www.coats.com

SULKY
Metallic and Rayon Threads
http://www.sulky.com

YLI
Metallic Serger Threads
http://www.ylicorp.com

AMERICAN & EFIRD INC.
Signature and Mettler Threads
http://amefird.com

FIBERFILL AND FUSIBLES

PELLON
Fusible Interfacing
http://www.shoppellon.com

THE WARM CO.
Steam-A-Seam and Fusible Fleece
http://www.warmcompany.com

FAIRFIELD PROCESSING
Poly-Fil
http://www.poly-fil.com/quiltprojects.asp

HOBBS
Fiberfill
http://www.hobbsbondedfibers.com/craft.html

AIRTEX
Fiberfill
http://www.airtex.com

Sewing Machines

Baby Lock
Sewing Machine
http://www.babylock.com

Brother
Sewing Machine
http://www.brother-usa.com

Simplicity
Sewing Machine
http://www.simplicitysewing.com

Janome
Sewing Machine
http://www.janome.com

Fabric Trims

Expo International
Trims
http://www.expointl.com

Robert Kaufman Company, Inc
Fabric
http://www.robertkaufman.com

Wrights
Trims
http://www.wrights.com

Cathy Franks
Fabric Painting
www.cathyfranks.com

Lady Dye Fabrics
Fabric Painting
www.ladydyefabrics.com

A&A White's
Fabric
www.sew-fabric.com

Irons

Shark Euro Pro
Iron
http://www.euro-pro.com

Rowenta
Iron
http://rowentausa.com

Additional Resources

Annie's Attic
Web: www.anniesattic.com

Bernina of America
Web: www.berninausa.com

Clotilde LLC
Web: www.clotilde.com

Connecting Threads
Web: www.ConnectingThreads.com

Elna USA
Web: www.elnausa.com

Ghee's
Web: www.ghees.com

Herrschners Inc.
Web: www.herrschners.com

Home Sew
Web: www.homesew.com

Husqvarna Viking Sewing Machine Co.
Web: www.husqvarnaviking.com

Keepsake Quilting
Web: www.keepsakequilting.com

Kenmore
Web: www.sears.com

Olfa-North America
Web: www.olfarotary.com

Pfaff
Web: www.pfaffusa.com

Singer
Web: www.singerco.com

Tacony Corp.
Web: www.tacony.com

The Timtex Store
Web: www.timtexstore.com

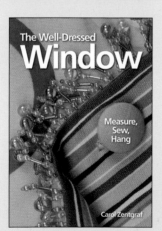
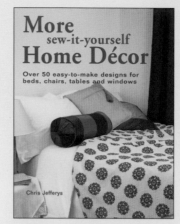